Lost Restaurants

OF

PROVIDENCE

Lost Restaurants

OF

PROVIDENCE

— DAVID NORTON STONE —

AMERICAN PALATE

Published by American Palate
A Division of The History Press
Charleston, SC
www.historypress.com

First published 2019

Manufactured in the United States

ISBN 9781625859303

Library of Congress Control Number: 2018966259

For my mother, who most misses Collier's Bakery on Broad Street and Corrigan's Fish, Chips & Grille on Prairie Avenue

Contents

CONTENTS

CONTENTS

Acknowledgements

In researching and writing this book, I have been grateful for and, at times, overwhelmed by, the banquet of memories served up by almost every Rhode Islander I questioned about favorite lost restaurants. This book contains a large but by no means complete list, and nothing was more valuable to me in deciding which lost restaurants to include than these often impromptu discussions. A lost restaurant is only worth writing about if it is missed.

Several restaurateurs have been especially helpful in providing details about the day-to-day challenges of running a restaurant in Providence, their culinary inspirations and the tastes of their customers. I am extremely grateful to Dewey Dufresne for speaking to me about his groundbreaking Joe's restaurants and for sending me on a hunt for Nance's mustard; to Anthony Salemme of Downcity Diner for sharing his history, as well as for the many happy meatloaf sandwiches of my youth (the recipe he provided for that meatloaf will now sustain me into old age); to Fred Goodwin, formerly of the Barnsider's Mile and a Quarter, whose current restaurant Bravo allowed me to experience a Hawkeye sandwich and does much to keep the tastes of lost Providence dishes alive; and to Don Bianco, steward of the memory of the Shepard Tea Room he once managed and who reminded me that a treasured dish, even one as simple as date nut bread and cream cheese, is as much about presentation as flavor.

For help with the images and menus in this book I am indebted to Christopher Scott Martin of Quahog.org, who writes brilliantly about the quirky food curiosities of his adopted state and has amassed a personal museum of Rhode Island history from estate sale finds, including the fortuitous discovery just in time of a Copper Galley menu. In addition to providing many of the images for this book, Christopher provided invaluable scanning assistance. Christine Francis of the pioneering Carmen & Ginger Vintage Goods shop in the historic Arcade was an early enthusiastic supporter of this book and turned up astonishing menu finds from Armand's and McGarry's as well as an old Chinatown postcard.

I am grateful to the Providence Public Library's Rhode Island Collection for its images and its marvelous typewritten Rhode Island index and *Providence Journal* card catalogue. Long live microfilm.

The exhibit and walking tour of Providence's Chinatown presented in 2018 by the Rhode Island State Archives was a long overdue examination of the Chinese American experience in Providence and greatly enriched this book's chapter on Chinese restaurants.

My family and friends have been generous with their restaurant memories and in all ways. In particular, I am grateful to Kevin Michael Sullivan; Emily and Robert Connolly; Christine Connolly, for advice on finishing the book; Earleen and David Small; Mary and Gary Herden; Susan Keegan; Jack Keegan; Michael Keegan; Janeen and Tom Stone, who fell in love at Luke's; Paulette and Rick Watkinson; Josh Stone; Janet Masse; and Stephen McGovern. My late grandmother Helen Stone animated restaurant history with her stories of honeymoon and chow mein sandwiches. My parents, Nancy and Al Samson, provided a comfortable, cat-filled (rest in peace, Lily) writing haven, and my mother was the earliest reader of this book, as she has been of everything I have ever written.

Introduction

This book is a history of Providence, told from the perspective of where and what its citizens ate.

Providence has always been a city with a celebrated food culture. The feast in these pages begins around 1890, when oyster houses and shore dinner halls serving the native cuisine of clams and oysters existed alongside restaurants specializing in German food, wine and beer. At the Pettis Oyster Rooms on Orange Street, former oystermen who still wore the red flannel undershirts of their trade under their white waiters' shirts served raw oysters from Pettis's wholesale place on South Water Street, milky oyster stews and authentic Rhode Island clam chowder with tomato. At the seaside sheds at Fields Point, thousands could be fed at a time on a Rhode Island shore dinner, famed worldwide for its price (fifty cents) and the dramatic procession of baked clams, corn, sweet potatoes and fish, accompanied by chowder, clam fritters, Indian pudding and watermelon. The smallest state, Rhode Island had a bit of a Napoleon complex, and the size of its meals and the number of people who could be fed at once were a marvel to visitors. Little state, big restaurants.

Insecurity could also be detected in the number of places that used the name of the great city to the south in their description, such as the New York Quick Lunch.

According to Welcome Arnold Greene, there were about eighty restaurants in Providence by 1886. Providence then was a place where gentlemen-only establishments prevailed and where the most popular cuisine was German

The Pettis name meant huge, delicious oysters in Providence. *Christopher Scott Martin/Quahog.org*

food, fare that would later evolve into our core American foods of hot dogs, hamburgers and beer. The city directory used the term *eating houses* rather than *restaurants*, and indeed, restaurants were still a relatively recent development. The first real restaurants in the United States, like Delmonico's in New York and the Union Oyster House in Boston, had been established in the 1830s. However, by the early 1900s, people in Providence were beginning to wax nostalgic about the portions and prices of bygone days, when a slice of deep-dish apple pie six inches high could be had for a nickel. In memory, the pies oozed juices and had a lattice crust that melted in the mouth.

Later, at a time when Providence was one of the most prosperous cities in America, downtown hopped day and night. Restaurants like Childs stayed open twenty-four hours to capture the late theater and nightclub crowds, and mobile carts set up to feed hungry workers on the night shift. Completing the Edward Hopper–esque night owl scene was the griddle chef in a tall white hat at Childs who stood in the bay window making pancakes and English muffin–like butter cakes (that recipe is included in this book, as well as several others from lost Providence restaurants). Fine dining was primarily French, and the Dreyfus Café was reputed to be the largest and best French restaurant in New England. The Dreyfus was so popular that it survived even through Prohibition when Gallic fine wines were no longer an option to accompany dinner. Places like Gibson's offered quick lunches served across the soda fountain counter.

VISIT
New York
Quick Lunch Oyster House.
And Live Like Millionaires at Very Moderate Prices.

THOMAS F. LAHEY, Proprietor.

17 Dorrance St.,   Providence, R. I.

The New York Quick Lunch Oyster House was actually in Providence. *Providence Public Library.*

No single person could represent Providence, but that did not prevent writer H.P. Lovecraft from declaring, "I am Providence." Every year, this statement becomes a little more accurate, as Lovecraft's worldwide reputation increases and fans flock to the city to see the places he wrote about in his fiction and to discover the landmarks important to him. Lovecraft preferred College Hill to downtown, which he considered a second-rate imitation of New York. However, it was downtown where he shared a memorable midnight meal with Houdini at the Waldorf Lunch, where he courted his wife, Sonia, at the restaurant in the Crown Hotel and dined in solitary splendor at the Shepard Tea Room.

This book is full of people who overcame adversity to realize their restaurant dreams. Flora Dutton ignored the disapproval of her teachers and discouragement of friends when she opened her Westminster Tea Room, soon attracting the business elite and acclaim, and her later café and restaurant Miss Dutton's Green Room became one of Rhode Island's most successful business enterprises. Miss Dutton was an early locavore, and her farm in Swansea, Massachusetts, provided the flowers and vegetables for her restaurant. Chinese restaurants in the city flourished despite the demolition of Chinatown and a failed petition by Providence's power brokers to bar Chinese restaurants from Westminster Street. The philanthropic Tow family of Port Arthur and Ming Garden prospered and became part of the new establishment of Providence. No one could resist Ming Wings.

During the Depression, Providence was nowhere near depressed, as kidney beans and toast kept bellies full. The saintly Frank Koerner of Koerner's

Lunch extended credit to everyone who asked, and the homeless were allowed in to keep warm with a nickel cup of coffee and sheltered from the frigid early morning streets. According to records kept for World War II rationing purposes, Koerner's Lunch fed three million people during that period alone.

Providence was keen to capitalize on the crazes sweeping the country, particularly after the end of Prohibition, when highly themed nightclubs and sophisticated cocktail lounges like the Beachcomber and the Bacchante Room convinced Rhode Islanders it was respectable to drink again.

Much of Rhode Island's classic vernacular cuisine was served by the lost restaurants described in this book. There were coffee cabinets, clam cakes and chowder, Saugy hot dogs with celery salt, snail salad and johnnycakes. But the really startling thing is how refined Providence restaurant cuisine has been throughout the years and how fresh and local the food. Hotels like the Narragansett, the Crown, the Dreyfus and the Biltmore (with its rooftop vegetable and poultry farm) set the tone, sourcing the best products even in wartime. Seafood palace Johnson's Hummock's Grill had its own lobster purifying tanks and scallop processing facility in Wickford. Almost every restaurant served Block Island swordfish.

The '60s changed everything. No longer did people put on white gloves to go shopping at the great department stores downtown for everything under the sun, stopping for a hamburger at McGarry's, date nut bread sandwiches with olive cream cheese at Armand's or a donut at Downyflake. Instead, they drove to the suburban malls. By the early 1970s, Johnson's Hummocks, Miss Dutton's Green Room and the Shepard Tea Room, indomitable giants of the local restaurant scene that had fed millions, toppled one after the other. There had been no greater threat to the Providence dining scene since the rise of the quick lunch in the early decades of the century, and perhaps the city needed to change. It was rumored that a black woman was denied service at Childs Restaurant.

How did Providence revive to again become one of the preeminent restaurant cities in the county? In 1914, Gertrude I. Johnson and Mary T. Wales founded a business school in Providence. The school's founders were focused on the practical application of knowledge. Johnson & Wales opened its College of Culinary Arts in 1973, offering two- and four-year programs in culinary arts, pastry arts, food service management and hospitality. The Johnson & Wales dedication to "what lies beyond" education meant that its students were not only preparing all the food for the university's dining halls but also apprenticing in Providence's restaurants and later opening their own establishments in the city.

While Emeril Lagasse may be the most famous of its culinary school graduates, many of the chefs of Providence's restaurant renaissance scene came from Johnson & Wales, and some, like Maureen Pothier of Bluepoint, have returned there to teach. The Rhode Island School of Design's creative culture also sparked restaurant excitement in Providence, even before the school offered a culinary program. Al Forno's George Germon and Johanne Killeen are both RISD graduates who began their careers working for Dewey Dufresne at Joe's Upstairs. John Rector was a Brown student who managed a RISD bar and later opened Leo's in the Jewelry district. In addition to serving cheap beer and the best chili in town, Leo's was a gathering place for the people who believed in downtown Providence and thought it was too cool and hip a place to leave, so they stayed and reinvented it.

The renaissance of Providence had plenty of fits and starts, just as it had Mayor Vincent "Buddy" Cianci, who advanced positive change in the city while the negative fallout from his administrations' scandals threatened to undermine that progress. Cianci's interaction with the restaurant community could be helpful, and he had excellent taste in food. Cianci even opened his own short-lived restaurant in the city, the *M*A*S*H*-themed Trapper John's. But in the case of Amsterdam's, when he was denied a table one night, the result was disastrous for the restaurant and ultimately the mayor.

Providence is credited as the birthplace of the diner, and no book about lost restaurants could be complete without discussing the Silver Top, Mike's Wagon or the Ever Ready. Unfortunately, it was paradoxically the renaissance of Providence that occasioned the demise of many of these open-all-night refuges.

A lost restaurant is most fundamentally not only one that no longer exists but also one that is deeply missed. We cannot bring them back, but they have shaped our existing restaurant culture and are still with us in that sense. Something that I constantly wondered about in writing this book is how many restaurants might have endured if they had been able to withstand the immediate challenges that led to their closing. Those challenges, however, were often insurmountable. There were demographic and social changes that profoundly altered where and how people chose to dine (Childs, Miss Dutton's, the Shepard Tea Room, Johnson's Hummocks). Sometimes, restaurants were such a perfect illustration of the American dream that there was no second or third generation interested in taking over (Eddie & Son). Most heartbreaking is when misguided notions of civic development or urban planning deem venerable and useful restaurants to be eyesores that need to be sacrificed for a more important project like a corporate headquarters or shopping mall (Mike's Wagon and the Silver Top).

As will be seen, there is lost and then there is really lost. Fortunately, in many cases, lost restaurants live on in the sense that their physical structures are used for new restaurants or other purposes. Perambulating the streets while researching this book, I found most places I wrote about still exist. It is my hope that this book will generate interest in and itineraries for walking tours of the lost restaurants of Providence. We lose more every day. In one dire week in the summer of 2018, the city lost three of its oldest and finest: Paragon, XO and the Cable Car Cinema and Café.

A brass plaque in front of Mee Hong on Westminster Street welcomed patrons with these words: "Through these doors pass the nicest people we know." We must continue to live up to that confidence by eating at our favorite restaurants.

1
Classics

MISS DUTTON'S GREEN ROOM RESTAURANT AND CAFÉ
1912–1965
44–48 Washington Street

Flora Eliza Dutton (better known as simply Miss Dutton) was one of the most successful Rhode Island food entrepreneurs of the twentieth century. Long before Martha Stewart came along, Miss Dutton understood that her farm and outdoorswoman lifestyle could help build a brand and that the brand could in turn support her lifestyle. But first she had to defy every mentor who advised her not to follow her dream of opening a restaurant in Providence.

Miss Dutton was born in Craftsbury, Vermont, and graduated from Simmons College. Her first job was as assistant director of a food shop in Boston, where she had a two-year contract and managed to deal with a difficult manager. The experience convinced her she could succeed in her own business, but a favorite professor at Simmons recommended she teach instead, and a good friend in Providence cautioned her that women did not often go out for lunch there. Over these objections, Miss Dutton and her early partner Agnes Best opened the Westminster Tea Room at 303 Westminster Street on October 31, 1912, and found immediately that there were many local businesspeople waiting for a restaurant like hers. Curiously, the 1913 city directory did not list the business as a restaurant but under the owners' names: Flora E. Dutton and Agnes M Best, tea room, 303 Westminster Street. Miss Dutton supplemented her income by teaching cooking. She was affiliated with the Providence Cooking School ("Instruction in General and Fancy Cooking"). A 1916 advertisement for the school invited interested parties to apply to Miss Dutton at the Westminster Tea Room.

In 1925, Dutton and Best opened a lunch counter at 48 Washington Street and, in 1928, opened the Green Room upstairs at 44 Washington Street, closing the Westminster Street location. The Green Room seated 165 people, and the downstairs lunch counter could serve 49. The Green Room sprawled over three floors and routinely fed 1,800 customers daily. The restaurant employed an average of 70 people. Katherine Dwyer was one of the first waitresses hired in 1912, and eventually 7 of her daughters waited on tables there. Everything was made fresh on the premises, from the pastries to the gravies. Miss Dutton's seventy-acre Westminster Farm and its twelve-room farmhouse in Swansea were extensions of the restaurant, providing flowers for the tables and vegetables for the kitchen in season. This farm-to-table ethos was seen even in the corporate cafeteria that Miss Dutton opened in 1934 for the *Providence Journal*. What did people love to eat at Miss Dutton's? The oatmeal bread, the mushroom soup and the popovers were all favorites, and her chicken on cornbread was considered unique and unable to be replicated. For the fortieth anniversary of her restaurant in 1952, Miss Dutton published a small book with ten of her most requested recipes, including the three-inch-high swordfish steak, which she slathered with mustard, browned in bacon fat or butter, then baked and basted with a sauce of melted butter, dill and lemon. A baked chocolate bread pudding also made the list. In 1954, Miss Dutton confessed that the most popular item at the restaurant was the seventy-five-cent luncheon special. People in Providence loved a bargain.

Surprisingly. Miss Dutton, despite having her name on the awning outside, was not a front-of-house personality, and many who frequented her restaurant had never spoken with her. But the public was fascinated by her, and she was the subject of frequent newspaper and magazine profiles. For example, Miss Dutton understood that gaining weight was an occupational hazard in her business, and readers ate up a newspaper story with the headline "Her Limit Is about 1,400 Calories a Day."

Miss Dutton retired in 1956 at the age of seventy, and the restaurant continued to operate with a few different owners. Patricia Dwyer (daughter of original waitress Katherine Dwyer) and her husband, John Tabella, took over the restaurant in 1962 and were its final owners. In a column that appeared in the *Journal Bulletin* in March 1965, writer John Hanlon, who had eaten many sustaining meals there, lamented that the Green Room had served its last on January 30. Its location in Providence at a time when downtown was in decline, the costs of operating a restaurant where everything was scratch-made daily, changing eating habits and a sense that Miss Dutton's gracious gentility was out of step with the tumultuous times all led to its demise.

In retirement, Flora continued to work at her farm, fished at her cabin in Rangely, Maine, volunteered at the Olde White Church in Swansea and spent time with her German shepherd Pal. Miss Dutton died in August 1984 at the age of ninety-seven, remembered as a woman decades ahead of her time in the city whose dining scene she once defined.

FIELDS POINT

1849–1910
Providence Waterfront

Ephraim Thurber held the first public clambakes at Fields Point in 1849, following in the tradition of the Narragansetts, who had first prized the clams and oysters of the gathering place they called Pumgansett. The point itself was named for Thomas Field, whose thirty-seven-acre farm occupied the site, and it was, in its heyday, a bucolic setting. The City of Providence ran a smallpox hospital there and leased part of the land to the clambake facility.

Just before the Civil War, the *Merrimac*, a side-wheel steamship, was tied up at Fields Point, and the clambakes that had been prepared on the beach were served in the comfort of the ship. This came to an end when it was discovered that gambling was being served for dessert, and the *Merrimac* steamed elsewhere. The clambakes then began to be served in sheds at Fields Point, and as the bakes became increasingly popular, one shed was joined to another, forming a dining pavilion. Thus was born Rhode Island's greatest and most famous contribution to the world of restaurants: the shore dinner hall. Narragansett Bay would later be lined with shore dinner halls from Providence to Block Island, including the world's largest at Rocky Point, but Fields Point was the first. Shore dinner halls were devoted to one thing, shore dinners, which were in turn based principally around one food item,

View of Narragansett Bay and Fields Point. *Author's collection.*

A clammy postcard depicting the world's first shore dinner hall at Fields Point. *Author's collection.*

steamer clams, strewn with seaweed and baked over hot stones, served with a few other additions. Russell Fenner succeeded Thurber at Fields Point, and his shore dinners consisted of baked clams, clam cakes, clam chowder (with tomatoes added), sweet potatoes, baked bluefish, sliced onions and cucumbers, watermelon, Indian pudding and more baked clams.

Fields Point reached its zenith of popularity under Colonel S.S. Atwell, who ran it from about 1887 to 1910. Fields Point offered the nearest clambakes to the city, and workers could visit for their lunches. The facility served fresh bakes every day at 12:30 p.m., 2:30 p.m. and 5:00 p.m. Fields Point was so popular under Colonel Atwell's ownership—especially on Sundays, when most other dining establishments were closed—that he had to enlarge the dining room until there was no more room to expand. This was one of the first manifestations of what would become an odd and frequently noted fact about Rhode Island. The smallest state offered some of the largest communal dining experiences in the country.

Some of the best-known bakemasters in the clambake trade got their start at Fields Point, among them Charles Lyon of Rocky Point and Thomas Crowell of Crescent Park. Crowell, who started working at Fields Point at age eleven, once divulged that one of his trade secrets learned there was to scorch the rockweed before sealing it in the bake.

The trinity of great shore dinner halls at Fields Point, Rocky Point and Crescent Park is depicted on this postcard. *Author's collection.*

Shore dinners at Fields Point came to an end in 1910 with the retirement of Colonel Atwell. Atwell auctioned the clam sheds, buildings, boilers and kettles in 1911. At the auction, which netted $1,100, the proprietor of the Rocky Point and Crescent Park shore dinner halls was an enthusiastic bidder on the equipment. There is a direct line from the fare served at Fields Point to the recipes familiar to millions from Rocky Point and Crescent Park, including the orange-red chowder that is unique to Rhode Island's amusement parks.

After a long period of industrial use, Fields Point was later the location of the Hawaiian-themed Copper Galley restaurant in the 1960s and now, appropriate to its storied association with clam bakes and shore dinners, is home to Save the Bay, the Narragansett Bay Commission and the Johnson & Wales Culinary Museum.

SCHEDLEY'S

1879–1932
197 Union Street

The long history of Schedley's in Providence began in 1879 when Bill Schedley opened a tavern in the basement of the Barnaby Building at the corner of Westminster and Dorrance Streets. The Barnaby store upstairs had originally been several feet above street level, but when the emporium lowered its floor, it came at the expense of Schedley's headroom, and the tavern moved to Union Street. Bill's younger brother Joe took over ownership in 1892.

Men (yes, only men) entered Schedley's through highly polished swinging oak doors. Mirrored windows outside obscured what was happening within. The food was originally cooked on a gas plate in the back, but in 1893 or 1894, accounts vary, the kitchen moved to the second floor. In 1907, Schedley's added a new bar and tables and chairs along with clubby oak paneling. The kitchen was also expanded in the renovation. After that, this Providence classic never changed again, except for a colored picture of a fox hunt that Joe added to the south wall.

Once occupying a crowded field of taverns like Harry McDonald's, the Senate, the Rathskeller, Dresden and Jacob Wirth, Schedley's served German fare and Ehret's beer for a nickel a glass. Anheuser-Busch and Narragansett were also available on tap. Joe Schedley insisted on generous portions, and meals were delivered from upstairs on a noisy dumbwaiter. The cuisine was just as unaltered by time as the décor. Popular specialties were the veal cutlet served with Delmonico potatoes, pigs' hocks and sauerkraut with beer, as well as good old franks and beans for twenty cents (a quarter with a beer) on Saturday nights when department stores stayed open until 10:30 p.m. Joe once bought caviar in kegs it was so popular and affordable. Sandwiches were served on rye bread cut on a slant for big slices.

Schedley's daily specials never changed. Monday, boiled dinner; Tuesday, beef stew; Wednesday, fish chowder or veal kidneys and mushrooms; Thursday, ham and cabbage; Friday, fish of the day; and Saturday, roast fowl. It was not unusual to see college men studying at the bar. In fact, a strategically placed ad in the 1932 Providence College *Alembic* asserted, "Here is a fact every P.C. man should know. For real good food the two best places to eat are the St. Regis restaurant and Schedley's."

Schedley's retained its popularity even during Prohibition, when other Providence taverns like Jacob Wirth shut their doors. However, during the Prohibition years, the hours were curtailed from 7:00 a.m. until midnight to a closing time of 10:30 pm. Another challenge Joe faced over the years was maintaining food quality, especially of the beloved cold boiled ham, slow cooked for three hours and then left standing in the water overnight. In the later days, Joe found it increasingly difficult to source good smoked hams instead of those artificially injected with smoke flavoring. Joe finally closed the business in 1932, conceding that the era of sit-down lunches had concluded.

GIBSON'S

1915–1953
The Howard Building, 81 Exchange Place

On a trip to Cleveland, Ohio, Providence pharmacist J. Fred Gibson ran into an old acquaintance who was managing a drugstore there. Gibson was flabbergasted to see that his friend was selling sandwiches to customers right over the counter and immediately sensed that this direct service from counter to customer was going to be the next big innovation in the food world. By 1900, quick lunches, including those sold at Gibson's drugstores in Providence, were beginning to redefine how food was served and consumed in Providence.

Born in Massachusetts, Fred Gibson moved to Rhode Island in the late 1870s and took over a pharmacy on College Hill in 1889. By 1915, according to an advertisement, Gibson had seven stores in Providence, including a new showplace in the Howard Building on Exchange Place, directly across from Union Station. The new location was billed as an excellent place "to enjoy a cooling drink or a light lunch, as well as to secure a supply of GIBSON'S FAMOUS PROVIDENCE-MADE CHOCOLATES before taking your car home." Streetcar, that is. The importance of Gibson's as the manufacturer of the most popular chocolates in Providence at that time was made evident by Gibson's sign, viewable from the train station, announcing the availability of chocolates and bonbons in large letters. Gibson's filled its store windows with tin toy trucks, loaded with a pound of chocolates, and printed with the Gibson's Chocolates logo on the side. The toy and chocolates sold for fifty cents, and long after the chocolate was gone, the truck reminded its young owner of where more could be obtained. The store also did a brisk trade in cigars made in Tampa as well as in sodas and ices.

After Fred Gibson died in 1933, Fred H. Barrows was elected president of Gibson's Inc. Barrows rose to that position from a humble start as an assistant pharmacist in the 1890s and was associated with the company for fifty years. Barrows served as president of the Retail Confectioners Association of the United States and was instrumental in transforming Gibson's from a pharmacy into a successful chain of restaurants.

A menu from July 9, 1934, reveals an astonishingly wide selection of options for a quick-service restaurant. There is so much seafood on offer that Gibson's nearly qualifies as a clam shack and confidently announces its Rhode Island coastal setting. Broiled swordfish with parsley butter, broiled scrod, lobster salad sandwich (toasted), fried clams, scallops and sole, described with adjectives like "shore" and "fresh," tempted the gourmand with a taste for fare from Narragansett Bay. The menu also appealed to diners in the mood for traditional Yankee fare like roast Vermont turkey and dressing with cranberry jelly, New England boiled dinner, cold meatloaf with potato salad, Welsh rarebit on toast and chicken croquettes.

I first heard about Gibson's from my paternal grandmother, Helen Connolly Stone, who could thriftily dine there on her lunch break from Western Union downtown in the early forties. She was on her way to Gibson's for a honeymoon sandwich on the day she first met my grandfather, a platinum-haired Seabee from West Virginia named Norton. The

Gibson's was strategically located on Exchange Place, where trolley lines, the train station and city hall converged, and was especially busy on civic celebration days. *Providence City Archives.*

honeymoon sandwich derived its name from its sole ingredient lettuce ("let us alone") with a bit of mayonnaise on bread. The ten-cent honeymoon was the least expensive sandwich to be found at Gibson's, but apparently the nickname was too racy for a family establishment. On the menu, it is simply called "Lettuce Salad . . .10."

A woman writing to the *Providence Journal* recalled going to Gibson's as a teenager when it was to her a miniature Grand Central, the hub of Providence, where all the buses and trolleys stopped. The big windows looking out on the plaza allowed one to keep a lookout for friends. "Meet you at Gibson's" was an unofficial slogan, so often were those words spoken. There was once a large, four-sided square advertising clock at the corner of Exchange Place and Dorrance Streets, as famous a meeting place as the Shepard's Clock, where, whatever the actual time, it was "Time for Gibson's" according to the logo above the glass faces. At Gibson's, workers and shoppers could order coffee and English muffins and comfortably smoke while waiting for the trolley. There was a twenty-five-cent minimum for

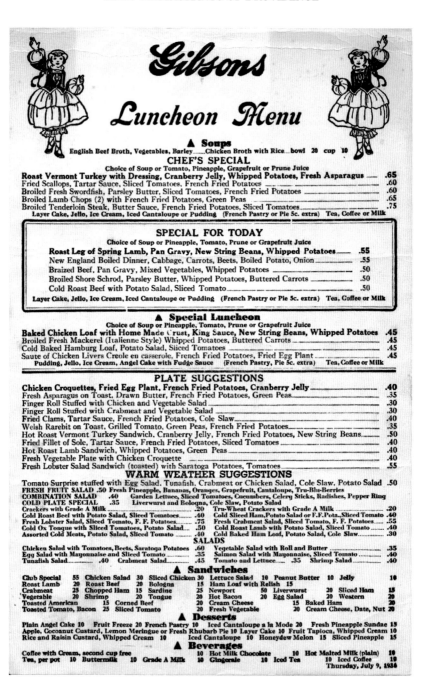

Gibsons

Luncheon Menu

▲ Soups

English Beef Broth, Vegetables, Barley......Chicken Broth with Rice...bowl 20 cup 10

CHEF'S SPECIAL

Choice of Soup or Tomato, Pineapple, Grapefruit or Prune Juice

Roast Vermont Turkey with Dressing, Cranberry Jelly, Whipped Potatoes, Fresh Asparagus	.65
Fried Scallops, Tartar Sauce, Sliced Tomatoes, French Fried Potatoes	.60
Broiled Fresh Swordfish, Parsley Butter, Sliced Tomatoes, French Fried Potatoes	.60
Broiled Lamb Chops (2) with French Fried Potatoes, Green Peas	.65
Broiled Tenderloin Steak, Butter Sauce, French Fried Potatoes, Sliced Tomatoes	.75

Layer Cake, Jello, Ice Cream, Iced Cantaloupe or Pudding   (French Pastry or Pie 5c. extra)   Tea, Coffee or Milk

---

SPECIAL FOR TODAY

Choice of Soup or Pineapple, Tomato, Prune or Grapefruit Juice

Roast Leg of Spring Lamb, Pan Gravy, New String Beans, Whipped Potatoes	.55
New England Boiled Dinner, Cabbage, Carrots, Beets, Boiled Potato, Onion	.55
Braized Beef, Pan Gravy, Mixed Vegetables, Whipped Potatoes	.50
Broiled Shore Schrod, Parsley Butter, Whipped Potatoes, Buttered Carrots	.50
Cold Roast Beef with Potato Salad, Sliced Tomato	.50

Layer Cake, Jello, Ice Cream, Iced Cantaloupe or Pudding   (French Pastry or Pie 5c. extra)   Tea, Coffee or Milk

---

▲ Special Luncheon

Choice of Soup or Pineapple, Tomato, Prune or Grapefruit Juice

Baked Chicken Loaf with Home Made Crust, King Sauce, New String Beans, Whipped Potatoes	.45
Broiled Fresh Mackerel (Italienne Style) Whipped Potatoes, Buttered Carrots	.45
Cold Baked Hamburg Loaf, Potato Salad, Sliced Tomatoes	.45
Saute of Chicken Livers Creole en casserole, French Fried Potatoes, Fried Egg Plant	.45

Pudding, Jello, Ice Cream, Angel Cake with Fudge Sauce   (French Pastry, Pie 5c. extra)   Tea, Coffee or Milk

---

PLATE SUGGESTIONS

Chicken Croquettes, Fried Egg Plant, French Fried Potatoes, Cranberry Jelly	.40
Fresh Asparagus on Toast, Drawn Butter, French Fried Potatoes, Green Peas	.35
Finger Roll Stuffed with Chicken and Vegetable Salad	.30
Finger Roll Stuffed with Crabmeat and Vegetable Salad	.30
Fried Clams, Tartar Sauce, French Fried Potatoes, Cole Slaw	.40
Welsh Rarebit on Toast, Grilled Tomato, Green Peas, French Fried Potatoes	.35
Hot Roast Vermont Turkey Sandwich, Cranberry Jelly, French Fried Potatoes, New String Beans	.50
Fried Fillet of Sole, Tartar Sauce, French Fried Potatoes, Sliced Tomatoes	.40
Hot Roast Lamb Sandwich, Whipped Potatoes, Green Peas	.40
Fresh Vegetable Plate with Chicken Croquette	.40
Fresh Lobster Salad Sandwich (toasted) with Saratoga Potatoes, Tomatoes	.55

WARM WEATHER SUGGESTIONS

Tomato Surprise stuffed with Egg Salad, Tunafish, Crabmeat or Chicken Salad, Cole Slaw, Potato Salad .50
FRESH FRUIT SALAD .50 Fresh Pineapple, Bananas, Oranges, Grapefruit, Cantaloupe, Tru-Blu-Berries
COMBINATION SALAD   .40   Garden Lettuce, Sliced Tomatoes, Cucumbers, Celery Sticks, Radishes, Pepper Ring
COLD PLATE SPECIAL   .35   Liverwurst and Bologna, Cole Slaw, Potato Salad

Crackers with Grade A Milk .20	Tru-Wheat Crackers with Grade A Milk .20
Cold Roast Beef with Potato Salad, Sliced Tomatoes .40	Cold Sliced Ham, Potato Salad or F.F.Pota.,Sliced Tomato .40
Fresh Lobster Salad, Sliced Tomato, F. F. Potatoes .75	Fresh Crabmeat Salad, Sliced Tomato, F. F. Potatoes .55
Cold Ox Tongue with Sliced Tomatoes, Potato Salad .50	Cold Roast Lamb with Potato Salad, Sliced Tomato .40
Assorted Cold Meats, Potato Salad, Sliced Tomato .40	Cold Baked Ham Loaf, Potato Salad, Cole Slaw .30

SALADS

Chicken Salad with Tomatoes, Beets, Saratoga Potatoes .60		Vegetable Salad with Roll and Butter	.35
Egg Salad with Mayonnaise and Sliced Tomato .35		Salmon Salad with Mayonnaise, Sliced Tomato	.40
Tunafish Salad .40	Crabmeat Salad .45	Tomato and Lettuce .35 Shrimp Salad	.40

▲ Sandwiches

Club Special 55	Chicken Salad 30	Sliced Chicken 30	Lettuce Salad 10	Peanut Butter 10 Jelly 10
Roast Lamb 20	Roast Beef 20	Bologna 15	Ham Loaf with Relish 15	
Crabmeat 25	Chopped Ham 15	Sardine 25	Newport 50	Liverwurst 20 Sliced Ham 15
Vegetable 20	Shrimp 20	Tongue 20	Hot Bacon 20	Egg Salad 20 Western 20
Toasted American 15	Corned Beef 20	Cream Cheese 15	Baked Ham 20	
Toasted Tomato, Bacon 25	Sliced Tomato 20	Fresh Vegetable 20	Cream Cheese, Date, Nut 20	

▲ Desserts

Plain Angel Cake 10	Fruit Freeze 20	French Pastry 10	Iced Cantaloupe a la Mode 20 Fresh Pineapple Sundae 20
Apple, Coconut Custard, Lemon Meringue or Fresh Rhubarb Pie 10	Layer Cake 10	Fruit Tapioca, Whipped Cream 10	
Rice and Raisin Custard, Whipped Cream 10	Iced Cantaloupe 10	Honeydew Melon 15	Sliced Pineapple 15

▲ Beverages

Coffee with Cream, second cup free	Hot Milk Chocolate 10	Hot Malted Milk (plain) 10	
Tea, per pot 10 Buttermilk 10 Grade A Milk 10	Gingerale 10	Iced Tea 10 Iced Coffee 10	

Thursday, July 9, 1936

Gibson's luncheon menu from July 9, 1934. *Author's collection.*

booth service, however. (My grandmother would not have made the grade with her honeymoon sandwich.) Gibson's was sold to Joseph A. McGarry Sr. and his sons in 1953 and later operated under the McGarry's name in the same prominent location. The Gibson's clock came down in September 1953, at 12:35 p.m. according to a contemporary photo, its copper and brass works sold for scrap after plans to relocate it in Exchange Place and later at the Narragansett Brewery fell through.

Jane Phillips started waitressing at Gibson's in 1942 in order to pay her bills. She recalled that in those wartime days the restaurant was open on Thanksgiving and Christmas, and with nowhere else to go, servicemen would come in the morning and stay all day. She worked at Gibson's and McGarry's until 1985, forty-three years in all, a link to a time when a quick lunch served with heart was so much more than fast food.

JOHNSON'S HUMMOCKS GRILL

1944–1970
245 Allens Avenue

"Internationally Famous Since 1905," according to a company history, Johnson's Hummocks Grill started with a clambake in the village of Hamilton in North Kingstown and ended as a huge restaurant in Providence. For a good part of the twentieth century, there was no name more associated with a good clam dinner in Rhode Island than Johnson (and I don't mean Howard Johnson and its clam strips).

In 1905, Frank Johnson built the first permanent structure of a clambake facility he called the Hummocks on a sandy peninsula in the village of Hamilton just outside of Wickford. At first, there was just a roof resting on cedar posts covering long benches set on the bare ground, but by 1910, this had evolved into a shore dinner hall with the capacity to seat 1,400 diners. The Johnsons did not have the best of luck at that location. In 1926, a cigarette butt ignited a fire that destroyed everything except the Johnson family homestead. Frank's son Henry rebuilt, but the hurricane of 1938 caused another total loss, and a new pavilion after that lost its roof in another hurricane in 1944. Henry Johnson finally built a solid brick restaurant he named Johnson's Hummocks Grill at 245 Allens Avenue in Providence; it boasted a Lobster Room, with lobsters fresh from

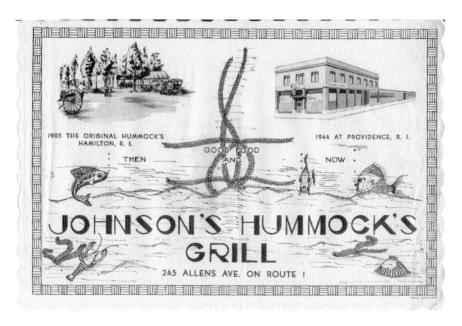

A placemat from Johnson's Hummocks Grill reminded diners that it all started with a clambake at the original Hummocks in Hamilton near Wickford. *Author's collection.*

Johnson's saltwater purifying tanks in Wickford. There was also a Neptune Room, a State Room, a Commodore Room and, for those lacking a taste for seafood, a Prime Rib Room. Johnson's Hummocks Grill never turned its back on its clambake origins (Henry Johnson even published a history called *It Started with a Clambake!*), and its menus announced on the cover, "Under the same management as the OLD HUMMOCKS at Hamilton Rhode Island."

Henry Johnson understood that the allure of his restaurant was derived from his access to the best and freshest Rhode Island seafood. To that end, he maintained a complex on the waterfront in quaint Wickford farther down Narragansett Bay, where the water was cleaner than in Providence. The storage tanks there, through which salt water pumped at the rate of one thousand gallons a minute, could hold forty thousand lobsters. This information was conveyed to diners on the cover of the menu, underneath an illustration of Johnson's pier in Wickford, along with the fact that sixteen thousand quarts of choice Rhode Island scallops were shucked there yearly, assuring a fresh supply to its patrons. A "suitable for framing" complimentary reproduction of the lobster and scallop shacks was available at the cashier's desk.

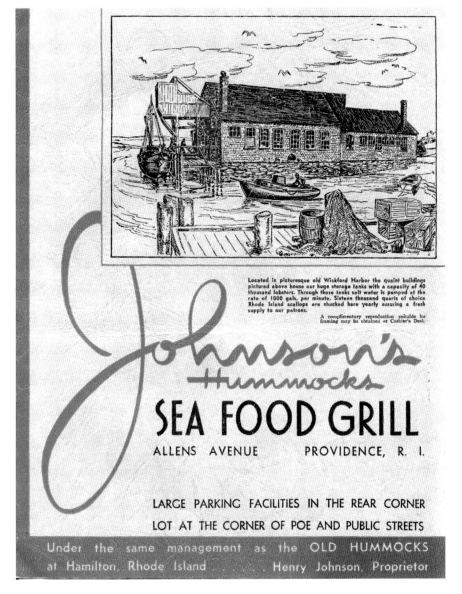

This Johnson's Hummocks menu cover from 1946 depicts the restaurant's lobster storage tanks in Wickford. *Author's collection.*

JOHNSON'S HUMMOCKS SEA FOOD GRILL
245 ALLENS AVENUE   PROVIDENCE, RHODE ISLAND

$1.35 -:- **DELUXE DINNER** -:- $1.35
(Dinners served from 12 Noon until 9 P. M.)
CHOICE OF
Little Necks or Juices
Also A Cup of
Soup du Jour, Rhode Island Clam Chowder or Clam Broth
ROAST STUFFED NATIVE CHICKEN
Giblet Gravy, Potatoes and Ready Vegetable

$1.15 -:- **DINNER** -:- $1.15
CHOICE OF
PLAIN LOBSTER MEAT   LOBSTER SAUTE
POTATOES

FRIED NATIVE SCALLOPS
Tartar Sauce, F. F. Potatoes, Cole Slaw

LOBSTER DINNERS
Hot or Cold Boiled, or Broiled Small Chicken Lobster $1.15
Hot or Cold Boiled, or Broiled 1½ lbs. Large Lobster $1.65

CHOICE OF FOLLOWING DESSERTS WITH THE ABOVE DINNERS
Ice Cream, Assorted Pies, Cake, Pudding, Chef's Cheese, Fruit or Coffee Jello
Coffee or Milk
Hot Tea, 10 cents Extra   —·—   Iced Tea or Coffee, 10 cents Extra

$1.15 -:- JOHNSON'S HOT LOBSTER COMBINATION TRAY -:- $1.15
CHOICE OF
LOBSTER SALAD, LOBSTER SAUTE or LOBSTER MEAT
OR
BROILED LIVE or COLD BOILED 1½ LBS. LARGE LOBSTER $1.65
Fried Oysters, Fried Clams, F. F. Onions, Potatoes and Roll

$1.75 -:- **DAILY DOUBLE** -:- $1.75
TWO BROILED LIVE SMALL CHICKEN LOBSTERS ON COMBINATION TRAY
Fried Oysters, Fried Clams, F. F. Onions and Potatoes

PLEASE PAY THE WAITRESS

APPETIZERS
Narganset Oysters .... .20
Little Necks (6) on Ice .... .15
Cherrystones .... .25
Shrimp Cocktail .... .30
Large Cherrystones .... .30
Seafood Cocktail .... .30
Lobster Cocktail .... .35
Chilled Hearts of Celery .... .20
Stuffed Olives .... .25
Celery and Ripe Olives .... .50
Prune or Apple Juice .... .10

SOUPS and STEWS
Clam Broth, Cup .... .10
R. I. Clam Chowder, Cup .10, Plate .... .15
Soup Du Jour, Cup .10, Plate .... .15
Chowder and Clam Cakes .... .25
Oyster Stew .... .35
With Cream .... .45
Little Neck Stew .... .35
With Cream .... .45
Lobster Stew .... .60
With Cream .... .70
Shrimp Stew with Milk .... .50
Scallop Stew .... .65
With Cream .... .75

FISH
Block Island Swordfish .... .50

LOBSTER and SHELL FISH
Broiled Live Chicken Lobster .... .75
Hot or Cold Chicken Lobster .... .75
Lobster Salad .... .40
Large Lobster Thermidor 1.25
Large Lobster Newburg on Toast 1.25
Lobster Saute .... .70
Plain Lobster Meat .... .70
Fried Lobster, Tartar Sauce .... .85
Lobster Stew .... .60
With Cream .... .70
Large Lobster, 1½ lbs. 1.25

SCALLOPS, OYSTERS and CLAMS
Fried Scallops .... .65
Broiled Scallops on Toast, F. Fries .... .85
Baked Little Necks, Casino .... .90
Baked Oysters, Johnson Style .... .50
Fried Fresh Clams, Tartar Sauce,
Potatoes, Cole Slaw .... .40
Steamed Clams, Cup of Broth .... .35
Steamed Little Necks, Cup of Broth .... .35

SALADS
Combination Salad with French dressing .... .35
Lobster Salad .... .60
Hearts of Lettuce, French, or
Russian Dressing .... .30
Chicken Salad .... .45
Tomato Surprise, Stuffed with Chicken .... .60
Stuffed with Lobster .... .60

DESSERTS
Chef's Cheese .... .15
Coffee or Assorted Fruit Jello .... .10
Pies and Pudding from our own
Pastry Shop, per order .... .10
Ice Cream .... .10

BEVERAGES
Iced Coffee or Tea .... .15
Cup of Coffee .... .05
Milk .... .10
Ginger Ale .... .10

50c — JOHNSON'S BLUEPLATE — 50c
Consists of
Fried Clams, Oysters, Scallops, Shrimp
and a Lobster Claw, Tartar Sauce,
Cole Slaw, Potatoes

75c -:- **CHEF'S SUGGESTION** -:- 75c
COMBINATION SEAFOOD PLATTER
Consists of
Piece of Halibut   Piece of Swordfish   Filet of Sole
Fried Scallops   Clams   Claw of Lobster
F. Fries   Cole Slaw   Cup of Coffee

Left: Lobster, scallops and clams starred on the Johnson's Hummocks menu. *Right:* Serving Bluepoint oysters, Block Island swordfish and chowder and clam cakes made with local quahogs, Johnson's Hummocks was an early locavore restaurant. *Author's collection.*

A basic dinner of lobster sauté or plain lobster meat, served with potatoes, cost $1.15 in 1946. For the same price, one could dive into a plate of fried scallops, served with tartar sauce, French fries and coleslaw. Dessert and coffee were included in the cost of these dinners.

Johnson's Hummocks offered plenty of turf to go along with the surf. A list of daily specials from February 3, 1946, proposed chicken okra, prime rib of beef au jus, roast stuffed native turkey with all the fixings, broiled sirloin with johnnycakes and the "extra specialty," a large order of fried frog legs.

For a really big night out, $1.75 bought the "Daily Double," two broiled small chicken lobsters in a combination tray with fried oysters, fried clams and French fried onion rings and potatoes. Another popular choice was the miniature clambake, hearkening back to a venerable Rhode Island shore dinner tradition. This began with a cup of chowder, followed by a whole boiled lobster, steamed clams, clam cakes, drawn butter, French fries and ice cream. The price of this feast was $1.50, which may have seemed steep to old-timers who could still remember when a full shore dinner with even more courses could be obtained in numerous places along the bay for $0.50.

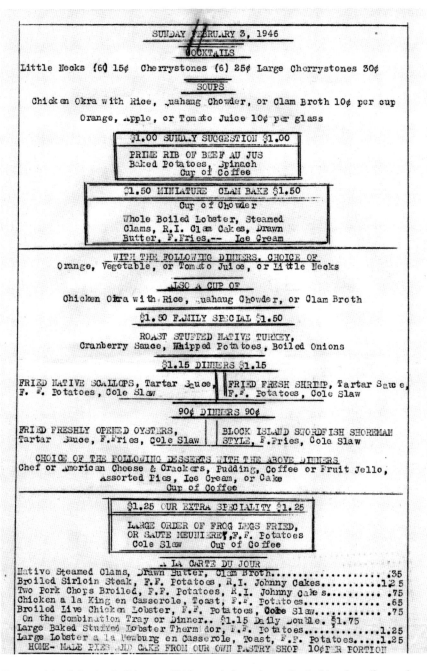

SUNDAY FEBRUARY 3, 1946

COCKTAILS

Little Necks (6) 15¢   Cherrystones (6) 25¢   Large Cherrystones 30¢

SOUPS

Chicken Okra with Rice, Quahaug Chowder, or Clam Broth 10¢ per cup

Orange, Apple, or Tomato Juice 10¢ per glass

$1.00 SUNDAY SUGGESTION $1.00

PRIME RIB OF BEEF AU JUS
Baked Potatoes, Spinach
Cup of Coffee

$1.50 MINIATURE CLAM BAKE $1.50

Cup of Chowder

Whole Boiled Lobster, Steamed
Clams, R.I. Clam Cakes, Drawn
Butter, F.Fries.-- Ice Cream

WITH THE FOLLOWING DINNERS, CHOICE OF
Orange, Vegetable, or Tomato Juice, or Little Necks

ALSO A CUP OF
Chicken Okra with Rice, Quahaug Chowder, or Clam Broth

$1.50 FAMILY SPECIAL $1.50

ROAST STUFFED NATIVE TURKEY,
Cranberry Sauce, Whipped Potatoes, Boiled Onions

$1.15 DINNERS $1.15

FRIED NATIVE SCALLOPS, Tartar Sauce,   FRIED FRESH SHRIMP, Tartar Sauce,
F. F. Potatoes, Cole Slaw   F.F. Potatoes, Cole Slaw

90¢ DINNERS 90¢

FRIED FRESHLY OPENED OYSTERS,   BLOCK ISLAND SWORDFISH SHOREMAN
Tartar Sauce, F.Fries, Cole Slaw   STYLE, F.Fries, Cole Slaw

CHOICE OF THE FOLLOWING DESSERTS WITH THE ABOVE DINNERS
Chef or American Cheese & Crackers, Pudding, Coffee or Fruit Jello,
Assorted Pies, Ice Cream, or Cake
Cup of Coffee

$1.25 OUR EXTRA SPECIALITY $1.25

LARGE ORDER OF FROG LEGS FRIED,
OR SAUTE MEUNIERE,F.F. Potatoes
Cole Slaw   Cup of Coffee

A LA CARTE DU JOUR
Native Steamed Clams, Drawn Butter, Clam Broth.....................35
Broiled Sirloin Steak, F.F. Potatoes, R.I. Johnny Cakes..........125
Two Pork Chops Broiled, F.F. Potatoes, R.I. Johnny Cakes...........75
Chicken a la King en Casserole, Toast, F.F. Potatoes..............65
Broiled Live Chicken Lobster, F.F. Potatoes, Cole Slaw............75
On the Combination Tray or Dinner.. $1.15 Daily Double. $1.75
Large Baked Stuffed Lobster Thermidor, F.F. Potatoes.............1.25
Large Lobster a la Newburg en Casserole, Toast, F.F. Potatoes.....1.25
HOME- MADE PIES AND CAKE FROM OUR OWN PASTRY SHOP 10¢ PER PORTION

The specials of the day in February 1946 rounded out the seafood with prime rib, a turkey dinner and even fried frog legs. *Author's collection.*

A Johnson's Hummocks postcard depicts two popular specials, the Daily Double and the "Miniature" Clambake. *Warwick Historical Society.*

Once Route 95 was built, the restaurant could easily be spotted due to its large sign facing the highway, and there are still many people whose idea of a perfect night out would be dinner at the Hummocks followed by a movie at the nearby Shipyard Drive-In. However, Johnson's Hummocks closed its doors suddenly on May 19, 1970, finally done in not by fire, wind or water but by suburban flight and a perhaps not mistaken impression that the location on the waterfront was crime-ridden. The restaurant had by that time been sold out of the Johnson family to out-of-state investors in the 1960s.

A restaurant as popular and long-lived as Johnson's Hummocks Grill naturally had far-reaching influence in Providence. A summer theater at the restaurant was operated by Betsy Argo, one of the founders of what would later become Trinity Repertory Company. In a way, the Johnson's Hummocks building is still involved in theater. It now houses a strip club. Dominican entrepreneurs Josefina "Dona Fefa" Rosario and her husband, Tony, found work at Johnson's Hummocks when they first moved to Rhode Island, she as a salad lady and he as a cook, allowing them to open their own business, Fefa's Market, which many credit as the first Latino restaurant in Providence. My own maternal grandmother, Amelia Martin, worked as a waitress at Johnson's Hummocks, and her daughters distinctly remember the lobster pin she proudly wore on her uniform when she left their South Providence home to work at Rhode Island's finest seafood restaurant.

DREYFUS FRENCH RESTAURANT

1900–1970
121 Washington Street

Café Dreyfus was known as the finest French restaurant in Providence at a time when American restaurants with the highest aspirations, like Delmonico's in New York, looked to France for their chefs, menus and wine. Arthur Dreyfus was born in Besançon, France, on June 17, 1862, and came to the United States when he was fifteen. By 1892, he had opened his first restaurant and hotel in Boston at Hayward Place, followed by a second hotel and restaurant in Providence in 1900, at the corner of Mathewson and Washington Streets.

A menu from 1901 reveals that the Dreyfus was firmly located in the Delmonico's tradition of French fare with an American accent. From

Hotel Dreyfus

French Restaurant

Hayward Place,
Boston.

Mathewson and Washington Streets,
Providence.

⁂

Table d'Hote, $1.00,
(With Pint of Imported Wine.)

⁂

Special Dinner on Sundays and Holidays.

⁂

A La Carte at all Hours.

The menu of Hotel Dreyfus French Restaurant was decorated with a grapevine to remind diners to order imported French wine to complement their dinners. *New York Public Library.*

11:00 a.m. to 3:00 p.m. and from 5:00 p.m. to 8:30 p.m., the Dreyfus offered a table d'hôte (*prix fixe* menu) for one dollar with a pint of imported wine. Oysters were available raw for fifty cents a dozen or could be ordered fried in bread crumbs and butter, roasted in the shell or in a stew or pan roast. Onion soup with cheese was French comfort food even then and is listed in English along with mock turtle soup and chicken okra. Lobster could be ordered "plain" (presumably steamed), broiled for sixty cents or in the house's special preparation à la Dreyfus for seventy-five cents. Fried smelts with "tartare" sauce were just as expensive as lobster even though they are an inexpensive appetizer option at places like Cranston's Twin Oaks today. The sirloin steak could be prepared and sauced fourteen ways, including, with a nod to French history, à la Béarnaise, Trianon, Victor Hugot (cute misspelling), Mirabeau and Richelieu. Demonstrating the kitchen's virtuosity, the menu offered everything from calf's head, brains and livers to veal cutlet with tomato sauce or Maryland fried chicken. Dessert options were surprisingly limited. There were apple fritters, crêpes (identified on the menu as French pancakes) with jelly, mendiants (chocolate circles with designs of fruits and nuts representing the monastic orders) and ice cream, but no mousses, soufflés or baked Alaska. Dreyfus offered a special crème de menthe for twenty-five cents. The menu further stated that guests would confer a favor on the proprietor by reporting any inattention on the part of the waiters and that meals could be served in sleeping rooms for twenty-five cents extra. A 1910 reference guide to Providence called Café Dreyfus "an admirable and typical French café." Specials in 1908 included broiled live lobster or Welsh Rarebit with a mug of Musty Ale.

One of the best-known waiters in Rhode Island restaurants, John F. Cribben, worked as a taproom waiter at the Dreyfus until just before his death. Cribben was famed for his amazing memory for names, faces and favorite tables of guests, even those he had not served for several years.

During World War II, the Dreyfus offered dinner and dancing in a club called the Shelter. After the deadly Cocoanut Grove nightclub fire in 1942, the basement bar at the Dreyfus closed as a safety measure.

Late in life, Arthur Dreyfus built a home on Dean Parkway in Cranston, and he had not lived there long before he passed away after a six-month illness in his seventy-sixth year. His children Harry and Edmund succeeded him in running the hotel. Harry Dreyfus, while working as a waiter in the Café Dreyfus in Boston—popular with gay men in the 1920s—had an affair with a Harvard student that led to the Secret Court of 1920, a tragic storm of expulsions and suicides. The facts of that purge and the role Harry Dreyfus (who was not a Harvard student) played in it have only recently come to light. Undoubtedly, the sophistication of the Providence Café Dreyfus appealed to students and other city residents looking for kindred bohemian spirits.

The Dreyfus Hotel building is now owned by AS220, and another lost restaurant, Local 121, occupied the former Dreyfus French restaurant space in recent years. *Christopher Scott Martin/Quahog.org.*

The Dreyfus family sold the hotel sometime in the 1950s, and it continued to operate into the early 1970s. Joseph Paolino Jr. owned the building for a period and operated a nightclub and restaurant there called Marlowes. The Dreyfus then served as a dormitory for Johnson & Wales before being purchased by AS220 for artists' living spaces. From 2007 to 2017, another lost restaurant, the outstanding Local 121, with a menu featuring ingredients from local farms, fishermen and cheese makers, was located in the Café Dreyfus space and served my favorite clam chowder in Providence.

JACOB WIRTH CAFÉ

1890–1918
2-4-6 Garnet Street

Jacob Wirth was one of the six German Americans who founded Narragansett Brewing Company, and this fact alone guarantees him Rhode Island beverage immortality. Although the iconic Jacob Wirth German restaurant on Stuart Street in Boston is still an ongoing concern, it is reportedly currently for sale and closed temporarily after a fire. Few remember today that there was once a Jacob Wirth restaurant in Providence. Jacob Wirth Café opened in Providence in 1890, serving imported Rhine wines and German beer accompanied by cold cuts, ham and other appetizers. In the same neighborhood of Weybosset Street could be found the What Cheer Beer Garden, the Hofbrau of Max Otte and Widow Hoch's. Jacob Wirth Café was on the second floor of the building at the corner of Weybosset and Garnet Street.

Jacob Wirth was born into a family of wine growers with vineyards near Bingen on the Rhine at Kreuznach. After immigrating to Boston, he opened his first restaurant there in 1868. In both Boston and Providence, the formula was simple. Beer steins and bottles were the decorations, food was served on mahogany tables without tablecloths and sawdust covered the floors.

An advertisement announcing Wirth's Hof Brau House stated that with the limited means at hand, the management had attempted to give Providence a reproduction of a German inn of the Middle Ages, both inside and out. Wirth's Hof Brau Haus was a long, narrow building with the dining spaces on the second floor. There were two restaurants, entirely separated with separate entrances. At the Men's Café, a businessmen's lunch was served from 11:30 a.m. to 3:00 p.m. daily, featuring "German Style of Cooking." The Family Restaurant, on the other hand, served an à la carte menu at all hours, and no liquid refreshment was sold in the family restaurant without a meal. Even there, however, women were admitted only when accompanied by male escorts.

The Providence interests of Jacob Wirth were looked after by his brother Henry, and when Jacob died in 1892, Henry served as trustee of his brother's estate while continuing to manage the Providence interests. In 1901, Jacob's son Jacob Jr. left Harvard and assumed control of the Providence and Boston business interests. A colorful lithograph for Jacob Wirth & Co., wine merchants of Boston and Providence, indicates the importance of the

Jacob Wirth & Co. wholesaled imported German wine and bottled beer from its building on West Exchange Street. *Providence Public Library.*

wholesale end of the business and, indeed, Jacob Wirth had a substantial warehouse in the city.

German restaurants like Jacob Wirth suffered when the United States declared war on Germany in 1917, but diners understood that a restaurant like Jake's was American through and through. In any case, the building was in the crosshairs of the rapidly expanding Outlet Company department store on Weybosset Street. First the What Cheer Saloon between the Hodges Building and Wirth was demolished in 1914 and replaced by a five-story addition, around the same time that the other German restaurants on Garnet Street were demolished for additions to the store. The restaurant closed in 1917, and the Outlet leased the building to sell men's fashions, hats in particular. Finally, Jacob Wirth Jr. agreed to sell the building, which was demolished, prompting the *Evening Tribune* to lament on June 21, 1923, that "[t]he demolition of the small two story building at the corner of Weybosset and Garnet Streets marked the passing of a landmark which was famous in pre-Volstead days…a gathering place for the elite of the beer imbibing fraternity."

SHEPARD TEA ROOM

1892–1974
122 Mathewson Street

The Shepard Company was a department store that provided all the necessities (and luxuries) of life under one roof, including groceries and shellfish. This self-sufficient mandate meant that the Shepard Company also required a restaurant. Founder John Shepard Jr. saw his enterprise less as one department store than as a collection of sixty stores and restaurants that were each managed individually. The original dining room of the Shepard Company was the Wellington Restaurant, which opened in November 1901 as a first-class establishment with two private dining rooms and elegant wainscoting, managed by Richard F Butler. The Wellington was located on the second floor of the Union Street side of the Shepard Company and was entered from a semicircular driveway whose remains can still be detected along Union Street. The Wellington was designed to compete with the greatest hotel restaurants of New York and Boston, but the Shepard Company also had a second restaurant to cater to those with simpler tastes.

A 1913 advertisement in the *Rotarian* assured readers that the Shepard's Restaurant and Tea Room was an approved establishment that served lunch to hundreds of business people and shoppers daily and had unexcelled cuisine, excellent service and moderate prices. There was music daily during luncheon and on Saturday nights when supper was served until 8:00 p.m. This advertisement is one of the earliest specific references to a tearoom at the Shepard Company, and it appears that at the time, tea was served on Monday, Wednesday and Friday, along with musical accompaniment.

In 1920, the Shepard Company acquired the Casino, a movie theater located at 122 Mathewson Street, and converted the building to serve as a standalone home for a cafeteria on the first floor and a fine-dining restaurant, the Colonial Room, on the second floor. The first radio station in Rhode Island, WEAN, was launched by the Shepard family in 1922 and broadcast from the third floor of 122 Mathewson Street, even occasionally featuring music played in the Colonial Room as part of its programming. Recordings of hits like "Where's My Sweetie Hiding?" and "Tell Me, Dreamy Eyes" by N.J. Perley Breed's Shepard Colonial Orchestra can still be heard online. Live broadcasts from the restaurant drew diners curious to see the voices from the radio and undoubtedly increased the popularity of the afternoon tea, as well as the sale of radios within the store. After the radio station moved, the third floor became a narrow cafeteria and lounge for Shepard's workers until the store's closing.

The refined atmosphere and genteel cuisine was enjoyed by H.P. Lovecraft, who, in 1934, superimposed a self-portrait on a contemporary postcard of the Shepard Cafeteria. He drew himself seated alone at a table for four in the cafeteria with his hat on the seat beside him, his writing bag at his feet. He also drew a waiter struggling to carry a tray and another treat-laden tray at his own table in the process of being devoured by the very thin writer. It is not surprising that the impoverished Lovecraft frequented the affordable Shepard Cafeteria and derisively referred to the posh restaurant upstairs as the "neo" Colonial Room.

A renovation in 1939 added a long lunch counter and replaced the tables shown in the postcard with booths. It was likely at this time the name Shepard Tea Room was officially adopted and announced by a neon sign above the entry doors on Mathewson Street.

In the mid-1940s, the John F. Davis Company took over the management of the Shepard Tea Room for the Shepard Company, adding state-of-the-art electrical food preparation equipment. A lawsuit in 1946 revealed that there was some disagreement between the two partners about was who responsible for paying for all the extra electricity being used. Apparently, everything worked out because the John F. Davis Company continued to operate the tearoom for decades.

Don Bianco, the former manager of the tearoom, keeps its memory alive. After leaving Shepard's, he ran a corporate cafeteria for an insurance company using many of the Shepard Tea Room's recipes. He is currently writing a cookbook that will compile recipes of his favorite Shepard Tea Room dishes.

Bianco confirmed the configuration of the now-demolished Mathewson Street building that housed the Tea Room. Surprisingly, it is nearly impossible to locate interior photos of the Shepard Tea Room, its popularity and endurance notwithstanding. The tearoom was on the first floor, and it could be reached by two entrances, one on Mathewson Street and the other through a covered alley between the building and a side entrance to the department store. On the second floor, in the space once occupied by the Colonial Room, was the Shepard beauty salon, connected to the store by a bridge. The Shepard employee cafeteria and the Shepard production bakery (operated by the Davis Baking Company) were located on the third floor.

Bianco further recalls that during the 1960s until closing in 1974, there were 190 seats comprising booths, tables and counter seats. The tearoom employed thirty waitresses at that time. Although some recall a glowing wood interior, that may have been an earlier version. During Bianco's era, the interior had some very limited Formica-like wood grain at the cashier stations and the entrance. The interior was refurbished during his time, adding a drop-ceiling with hidden neon lighting around the counters, a soda fountain and perimeter booths. The booths were reupholstered in bright orange and gold leather-like vinyl. The walls were painted a peach color, and an artist was commissioned to paint murals on the long wall over the booths. Bianco remembers the lost murals as flowers in putty-colored vases. He and customers thought they were quite beautiful at that time, although painting them posed some logistical difficulties. Bianco arranged to cordon a booth at a time and had the artist work during the peak lunch time. The customers enjoyed the show.

One of the most missed Shepard Tea Room dishes is the chicken croquettes. Illustrative of the sometimes happenstance manner that favorite recipes are created, the chicken croquettes began as way to use the chicken skins left over from making chicken soup. The chopped skins were combined with ground chicken, potato powder and bread crumbs, formed into conical croquettes, dipped in flour, eggs and crumbs and fried. The croquettes were served with a potpie-reminiscent supreme sauce. Other dishes treasured by folks on nostalgia websites are the grilled cheese and tomato sandwich, baked macaroni and cheese with a slice of tomato on top and the vertiginous Pike's Peak sundae, which some called the Christmas tree sundae. There was breakfast with Santa Claus, but some believed the real Santa Claus was only at the Outlet. Children enjoyed selecting their treats from a refrigerator case, with the favorites being the Boston cream pie and strawberry chiffon pie. However, nothing more epitomized the whole white-gloved dressing up to shop experience than the date nut bread (see page 131 for recipe) and cream cheese sandwiches.

When the Shepard Tea Room closed in January 1974, it was as though a way of life in Providence had ended. The best department store in the city and its timeless tearoom were gone. Although the Shepard Company building has found new life as a college campus, the Shepard Tea Room was demolished to make a parking lot.

NARRAGANSETT HOTEL

1878–1959
Dorrance Street

Fronting Dorrance, Eddy and Weybosset Streets, the eight-story Narragansett Hotel was for many years the epicenter of the city's social life and scene of some of its greatest dinners. The hotel opened in April 1878, and its grand dining room was forty by ninety feet and twenty-seven feet high. There also was a lunchroom on the ground floor open to the public.

Huge austere old-master paintings decorated the public rooms, everything from pastoral scenes of lambs to semi-nude female bathers. The more risqué artwork occasioned a few scandals, such as an outcry when too much artfully draped flesh on one canvas in the bar was visible to passing trolley passengers or the time in 1947 when a rowdy convention-goer cut out a portion of a painting on the mezzanine, allegedly just the derriere.

For decades, the hotel was defined by the outsized personality of Max Zinn, who began his employment there as a busboy around 1919, became headwaiter in 1924 and ultimately served as director and part-owner until his death in 1952. George Winkler, of Winkler's Middle Street Steak House, knew Zinn for decades and rated him the second-best hotel manager in Providence, narrowly surpassed only by Edmund Dreyfus of the Dreyfus Hotel. Tellingly, Winkler waited until 1953, after Zinn had died, to open his steakhouse because he knew he could never have competed with Zinn's Narragansett Hotel in its prime. Zinn loved food and procured the best for the Narragansett.

A menu from Halloween 1912, from the collection of the New York Public Library, is decorated with a witch on a broomstick and a pumpkin and reveals a succession of courses of extraordinary sophistication, including Imperial Squab a la Broche. (By way of contrast, decades later, when the Red Rooster in North Kingstown started serving squabs, they had to be called "little chickens" on the menu to convince people to order them.) Reflecting the hotel's location by the sea, Lobster Gratinee Narragansett was served, as well as a devilish Tartine Diablee and a frightful Salad Hallow E'en. The inconsistent mixture of French and English on the menu was common for the time, although perhaps revealing some provincialism.

Alcohol kept flowing at the hotel during Prohibition. During the hurricane of 1938, water flowed as well, filling the main dining room and floating tables through it. The Tap Room had eight feet of water, and

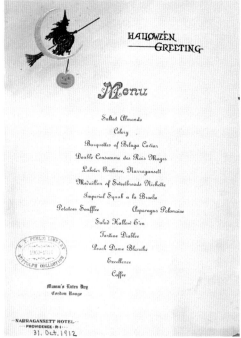

Above: A view of the Narragansett Hotel's Dorrance Street entrance. *Providence Public Library.*
Left: The menu from the 1912 Halloween dinner at the Narragansett Hotel. *New York Public Library.*

liquor stored in the cellar had to be discarded. World War II kept the hotel hopping, even though extra security guards were needed, as service members gravitated to downtown Providence for rest, recreation and romance. Despite wartime rationing, there were always steaks available at the Narragansett.

The kitchen would roast five hundred turkeys at Thanksgiving. At Christmas, there was caroling on the grand staircases of the hotel. Jewish community and business leaders gathered at the hotel between one and three o'clock every afternoon at what was known as the Narragansett Round Table. Many political dinners were held there as well, including one for Harry Truman, and the Narragansett was for many years the headquarters of the state's Democratic Party.

The Narragansett used the image of an Indian chief in its branding materials, along with the slogan "Where the Guest is King." The hotel once hosted a Native American wedding in what may have been a publicity stunt. However, the theming was far from consistent. In later years, the hotel lured customers to its Bar and Grille with promises that its low-beamed ceilings suggested an inn of the English countryside.

The hotel closed in 1959 and was later demolished to make way for Broadcast House, now a library for Johnson & Wales. At the time of the hotel's closing, it was reported that the lobby chandelier and rug were taken to the Hearthstone House in Seekonk. Bits of the hotel also survive at local estate sales; a friend recently purchased a blanket and pillowcase with the hotel's name on them.

CROWN HOTEL

1893–1962
208 Weybosset Street

Built in 1893, the Crown Hotel and its restaurants were an important presence in Providence for almost a century. Located on a busy stretch of Weybosset Street at the corner of Garnet, just down the road from the Outlet, the Narragansett Hotel, Jacob Wirth and the Gaiety Theater, the Crown Hotel announced on a sign painted on the side of the building that its restaurant was the most popular in town.

The Crown Hotel was on a vibrant stretch of Weybosset Street. *Providence Public Library.*

Writer H.P. Lovecraft was one of the Crown's restaurant's devoted fans. In fact, he wooed his wife there. Lovecraft dined at the Crown Hotel in September 1921 when Sonia Greene stayed there during her visit to Providence before they married, but apparently it also was the center of his writing activities. He described the Crown as "amateurdom's official headquarters in this village," in reference to his involvement with amateur journalism at that time. During their meal, Lovecraft eccentrically drank only a cup of very sweet, light coffee and ate some chocolate ice cream, indicative that Sonia should have known what she was getting into (their marriage was a short one). It was a compliment that Lovecraft would so heartily recommend a place downtown. Despite his adoration of College Hill, he thought of downtown Providence as merely a third-rate copy of New York. Perhaps his enthusiasm was because the Crown's dining facilities had very high standards of cleanliness.

Fred Mansfield, the proprietor of the Crown Hotel, was such a stickler for food safety that he wrote to the Providence Chamber of Commerce's Safety Committee inviting the members to visit his hotel's kitchen. The letter was later published in a 1914 issue of *Safety Magazine* and contained the impressive fact that all food workers were examined by a doctor twice a week:

Regarding the efforts made in the "Safety First" movement, I desire to state that outside of my own building, I have had no opportunity to devote any time to the subject thus far; but I am pleased to inform you that all employees of the Crown Hotel, coming into contact with food, either in its raw or prepared state, and all employees who handle crockery, silverware and glassware, are medically examined twice weekly by a reputable Providence physician. By employees, I mean all those who work in my kitchen, cooks and their assistants, dish washers, helpers, waiters and utility boys. I am also pleased to say that every piece of silverware, crockery or glassware is sterilized every time it is used, and every refrigerator in the Crown Hotel containing food or having anything to do with the keeping of food, is also inspected by a medical officer twice weekly.

Mansfield testified about the harmful business effects of Prohibition, not only on the Crown but to local liquor distributors. With the repeal of Prohibition in 1933, hotels opened beautifully decorated bars that would appeal to "respectable" women as well as men. The graciously decorated Deep Sea Cocktail Lounge at the Crown transported its guests under the sea with murals of mermaids and wave-patterned carpets. A diving suit stood at the entrance. Guests who could not swim could drink at the Crown's own entrant into the Tiki craze, the Beachcomber, where Zombies were served in a South Pacific décor. Paul Filippi, the successful Rhode Island restaurateur best known for Ballard's Inn on Block Island, got his start (and his stake for the Celebrity Club, opened in 1949, the first integrated nightclub in Providence, hosting black and white diners and jazz musicians) as a doorman at the Crown. He maximized his tips by quickly reading the names on luggage tags to impress traveling salesmen by greeting them by name.

A court-appointed receiver closed the hotel in 1950, and it was later bought at auction by members of the Chace family, who owned it until it closed in 1962. In the 1950s, for a cherry Coke or a steaming hot cup of coffee there was no place better than the new Crown Hotel Coffee Shop. Open daily from 7:00 a.m. to 2:00 a.m. for breakfast, lunch, dinner and light snacks, the Crown Hotel Coffee Shop was touted as the most modern in New England, and a color postcard reveals that it had the avocado-green counter stools, powder-blue blenders and bright-yellow napkin dispensers to back up that claim to ultra-modernity.

In the '50s, the Crown's dining theme changed from Beachcomber to staid. The Terrace Room aspired to be the smartest cocktail lounge in town, and the Georgian Room was one of two fine restaurants.

Above: The ultra-modern Crown Hotel coffee shop. *Left*: The Georgian Room and the Terrace Room resulted from a beverage and dining makeover at the Crown Hotel in the 1950s. *Author's Collection.*

A postcard from my collection mailed to a gentleman in Waxahachie, Texas, contains the following hand-typed message: "Coming to New England this year? The Crown Hotel is ideally located for a convenient stopover point." Presenting the postcard to the front desk on arrival would result in a 10 percent discount on the room rate.

The building was later purchased by Johnson & Wales and converted into the McNulty dormitory. The hotel's former front entrance was used as the Johnson & Wales bookstore. A fire damaged the building in September 1992 so badly that the roof caved in. The university decided to demolish the jewel that had been the Crown and used the land as part of a new campus.

2
Themed

THE RATHSKELLER

1914–1928
59 Eddy Street

A bohemian atmosphere right in the heart of Providence was supplied by the Rathskeller at 59 Eddy Street. Located to the rear of city hall, in the space later occupied by Luke's Chinese American Restaurant and down the road from where Haven Brothers sets up each night, the Rathskeller was the brainchild of John Scheminger Jr., who conceived of a themed restaurant for his hometown of Providence based on the famous Rathskeller of Germany. In the days when Germany was divided into minor states and provinces, cities like Hamburg, Bremen and Lubeck had independent governing bodies called Rat that conducted their business in the Rathaus. The cellars of these buildings contained elaborate eating and drinking places called, appropriately, Rathskeller.

Scheminger spared no expense in simulating the characteristics of these quaint historic places behind, though not in the cellar of, Providence's own seat of government. He employed the same color scheme, decorative design and oak paneling as in the Bremen Town Hall (now a UNESCO World Heritage site). Carved wooden effigies supported the mantels and cabinets in the restaurant. A collection of unique steins and pewter pitchers was arranged on the mantel above the paneled wainscoting. The light fixtures

The Rathskeller is visible behind city hall in this postcard of a patriotic human flag. *Providence Public Library.*

were made of wood and hung from the ceiling on wooden chains. The German Bar was illuminated in a subdued green glow, while diners in the main restaurant basked in a crimson radiance.

The ladies' restaurant was located downstairs, with booths large enough for families on both sides of the commodious room. A stringed orchestra provided a refined atmosphere during the dinner hours. However, the most miraculous innovation of the Rathskeller was that it had its own ice plant and refrigeration system. The only one of its kind in the state, the cooling system was such a novelty that it was displayed in a window on Eddy Street and became a tourist attraction of its own. The restaurant was said to be kept as cool and refreshing as an ocean breeze, even on the sultriest summer days.

The kitchen was just as modern and designed for instantaneous service in providing both the newly popular quick lunches or elaborate feasts. Max Otto, who had previously operated his own Hofbrauhaus, was the manager and was assisted by Frank Wiesbauer. It is significant to note that a restaurant owner could belong to the upper echelons of Providence society of that day. Scheminger, who was also the treasurer of the wine merchants Eddy and Fisher Company, was a Mason, Elk and club man belonging to the Providence Business Men's Association, the Pomham Club, the Rhode Island Yacht Club, the Edgewood Yacht Club, the Metacomet Club and the West Side Club.

The Rathskeller held an open house during the day on Tuesday, August 18, 1914, for guests to look over the building, but no food or drink was for sale. That night, at 7:30 p.m., Scheminger entertained city officials and movers and shakers at a dinner, and on the following day, the Rathskeller officially opened to the public.

In 1918, at a time when Germans and Austrians in the United States were regarded with suspicion, German restaurants were not immune to the anti-spy hysteria. An advertisement in the *Providence Journal* in October 1918 showed its patriotism by urging diners to buy war bonds in exchange for a free meal. By 1920, the restaurant's ads were promoting the following fancy, although not particularly German-sounding specials (referred to as "chow"): sweetbreads au Champignon, rice, asparagus tips; chicken patties à la Reine, green peas; veal steak sauté, stuffed tomatoes; or tenderloin steak, mushroom sauce, artichokes, green peas, julienne potatoes. Like many other German restaurants in Providence, the Rathskeller could not survive the war on beer known as Prohibition. A French restaurant, Old France, later opened in the space and was succeeded there by Luke's Chinese American Restaurant. Today, this storied location behind city hall hosts a bar called the Salon, but there is not a trace left of that German woodwork.

THE BILTMORE HOTEL

1922–1975
11 Dorrance Street

Over the years, the Biltmore Hotel has supported more themed restaurants hidden behind its Harvard brick walls than any other spot in Providence. While the hotel itself is still standing, all of its themed restaurants and bars, some of them from the years when the Biltmore was operated by Sheraton from 1947 to 1968, have been lost since 1975, when the hotel temporarily closed before reopening in 1979 as the Biltmore Plaza. The hotel opened in 1922, designed by Warren and Wetmore, who also were responsible for Grand Central Station and later the Royal Hawaiian Hotel (known alliteratively as the Pink Palace of the Pacific). Chef Charles Reidinger was engaged to oversee dining. Reidinger was chef on the steamer *George Washington* when it took President Wilson to Europe and had worked at hotels in Europe as well as at the Plaza and Biltmore in New York. Initially, the main dining room was of colonial type with blue, ivory and gold decoration. The less formal grill was Italian Renaissance in style, painted grey and silver. Both the restaurants and the kitchens were on the second floor. The hotel used gas for all its cooking, prompting it to publish a four-column announcement of this fact in an advertisement in 1922. The ad boasted that the kitchens were models of their kind, with over twenty gas ranges, broilers and ovens.

A pair of the Biltmore's famous Bacchante Girls, providing service with charm. *Author's collection.*

After the repeal of Prohibition in 1933, the Biltmore was no exception to a nationwide craze for creating lavish, themed cocktail lounges, lending an aura of respectability and elegance to the no longer illegal act of enjoying a drink. The Bacchante Room was one of the most unique bars in the country, featuring special hostesses called the Bacchante Girls, who wore short skirts with diaphanous netting over their legs.

With a sunken bar, piano music and service out of a Hollywood musical where one pressed a button at the table to call a hostess, the Bacchante Room was the height of sophistication. The floor was glass with pink lights underneath meant to show off the legs of the Bacchante Girls. However, looks were not everything, and the Bacchante Girls were known for their intelligent conversation with customers. Those who made it through the selection process were treated to weekly appointments with the hotel hairdresser and manicurist as well as taxi rides home. In 2011, the Biltmore searched for former Bacchante Girls in hopes of staging a reunion, and it was noted that there had been over two hundred of them through the years.

Amusingly, the Bacchante Room closed in the 1960s and was replaced by the Mansion House, a replica of a colonial tavern, and servers dressed in chaste colonial garb.

The Biltmore's Mansion House was a re-creation of a colonial tavern with servers in period garb. *Author's collection.*

Imbibers brushed up on their Shakespeare at the Biltmore's Falstaff Room. *Library of Congress.*

The fare from the Biltmore's themed Garden Room came from a rooftop garden providing the hotel with flowers, vegetables and, amazingly, chickens. There was even a plan for a dairy herd on the roof, but after what happened to the ducks (who escaped to Narragansett Bay in the 1930s), the idea was dropped.

The Biltmore's Falstaff Room, themed as a fifteenth-century taproom, was designed to appeal to fans of Shakespeare and was promoted as authentically English in every detail. This bar featured a mural portraying Falstaff, one of literature's most colorful and high-living characters, along with his imbibing friends. Prime Aberdeen Black Angus beef was served every evening at dinner. Prince Hal must have been paying.

The Biltmore promoted its other "famous rooms" in advertisements, including the Town Room ("good food, served in pleasant surroundings. Open for all meals"), the Jewel Box ("convenient street level cocktail lounge"), the Minute Chef ("handiest place in town for a delicious quick snack") and the Men's Bar ("a street level oasis reserved exclusively for males").

THE BEACHCOMBER

1940–1950
Crown Hotel, 208 Weybosset Street

Monte Prosser's Beachcombers were known nationwide for tropical food and exotic drinks, especially the Zombie (so strong they were limited to two per customer). Prosser was a nightclub promoter who eventually opened clubs of his own, ultimately employing a thousand people. At the 1939 New York World's Fair, Prosser operated a popular bar called Monte Prosser's Zombie. His first Beachcomber opened in New York City over the Winter Garden Theater, followed soon by the Providence location in the Crown Hotel and other outposts in Miami Beach, Boston and Baltimore. Tiki culture enthusiasts are miffed at Prosser because he appropriated for the East Coast, some say stole, a concept that had been pioneered by Don the Beachcomber in California.

The Beachcomber had an interior designed by Clark Robinson, who brought a jaw-dropping creativity and South Seas romanticism to his work. The block-long Miami Beachcomber designed by Robinson reproduced an entire Pago Pago street, including the sky. A souvenir photo of guests posing with elaborately costumed performers from the Providence Beachcomber reveals a fantasia of Polynesian-patterned wall coverings framed by bamboo. Many of the Providence customers were sailors and soldiers who had fought in the South Pacific and were nostalgic for its coconut trees and balmy breezes.

By 1941, Prosser had sold the Providence Beachcomber to the well-known Ruby Foo, whose legendary "Den" in Boston's Chinatown opened in 1929. A menu from Ruby Foo's Beachcomber shows a confident reliance on Chinese food. The $1.50 special included chicken noodle soup, Chinese roast pork and egg roll and the choice of half a fried chicken, chow mein (Cantonese style) or fried lobster Chinese style, along with Chinese candy and preserved "Gumquats." Large sections of the menu were dedicated to chow mein and chop suey, but sandwiches (chicken, cheese and club) could also be had with that Zombie. The Beachcomber did not tolerate freeloaders, and the menu cautioned "in order to provide good music and good wholesome entertainment, a minimum charge of $1.00 per person is necessary from Monday through Friday-Saturday and Holidays $1.50." That minimum charge meant that servicemen in uniform were often sparse at the 150-seat Beachcomber, although they thronged no-minimum hot spots.

There were three floorshows a night, at 8:00 p.m., 10:00 p.m. and midnight, featuring crooner Don Marco (his hits included "Gigolo Joe from Mexico" and "Chupa-Chupa") and six house showgirls dubbed the Beachcharmers. Dancer Jadim Wong both jitterbugged and impersonated Scheherazade.

In the aftermath of the Boston Cocoanut Grove nightclub fire on November 28, 1942, which killed 492 people, the Beachcomber closed briefly in December of that year to strip the interior of palms and bamboo matting. The flames that ignited the Cocoanut Grove were first seen in palm fronds. Even after losing some of that tropical decoration, the Beachcomber lasted until around 1950, when the Crown Hotel was taken over by new owners who remodeled it in the staid spirit of the Eisenhower years.

THE COPPER GALLEY

1960–1972
1 Washington Avenue

Overlooking "Millionaires Row," a panorama of expensive yachts along the Providence waterfront, and featuring Castaway Village where (the menu promised) your dreams of "white beaches and dusky hula maidens, tantalizing foods and exotic drinks" could come true, the Copper Galley was the conception of impresario Melvin Berry. Berry, who made his fortune with a chain of surplus stores and later purchased the vacant shipyard at the site of the historic Fields Point shore dinner hall, certainly spared no expense in making his dream of a Polynesian resort in Providence a reality.

The centerpiece restaurant was the maritime-themed Copper Galley, decorated with antique ship models and a collection of vintage copper ware. The Beachcomber Lounge featured picture windows overlooking the Shipyard Marina, itself a point of interest. Berry created his own Waikiki Beach by spreading tons of sugar-fine beach sand along the waterfront and dotting it with Kings and Queens cane chairs as well as Hawaiian-style huts made from bamboo and thatch. For swimming, there was an Olympic-size pool. To set the island mood, guests entered the complex through what the menu called "fountains of fire" and then crossed the bamboo "bridge of joy" to the insistent beat of drums. The menu consisted of the expected Polynesian temptations but also featured full Dall'Italia and Americana menus. Nowhere else did choices range from a cup of Copper Galley clam

The menu art for the Copper Galley depicts its location at Shipyard Marina as a bit of Waikiki on the Providence waterfront. *Christopher Scott Martin/Quahog.org.*

chowder, Tahitian onion soup and clams kai (stuffed with island spices) to clams casino. The globe-trotting menu somewhat threatened the theme, but it was meant to suggest the idea of a sea voyage.

Modern-day Tiki fanatics do not seem to celebrate the memory of the Copper Galley especially today, but it clearly had all the kitschy drinks, including a Pina Passion served in a pineapple, a Koko Loco served in a coconut, a Zombie (with recognition for the Don the Beachcomber original), as well as such other classics as the Maiden's Downfall ("stimulating for the broken hearted"), the Suffering Bastard ("a dirty stinker") or the Dr. Funk of Tahiti ("a truly Tropical drink originating in Papeete"). The special mugs these drinks were served in could be purchased for $1.50. When diners heard the Beachcomber's Gong, they knew someone had ordered the Royal Ceremony of the Islands, a drink that cost an astonishing $7.50.

Left: The Copper Galley's appetizer menu spanned the globe. *Right*: Dinner at the Copper Galley featured Polynesian entrées like Lobster Sayonara, Pineapple Veal Waikiki and Shrimp Bongo Bongo. *Christopher Scott Martin/Quahog.org*

Berry went on a spending spree at a sale of elements from the New York World's Fair of 1964 and 1965 after the fair closed for good in late 1965, collecting $1.5 million worth of stuff, including the entire artificial jungle for the Ford Pavilion, a pineapple garden, thatched huts and a volcano that erupted every six minutes, delivered to Providence in 130 truckloads from New York. Much of the Hawaiian pavilion was absorbed into Castaway Village at the Shipyard Marina. Berry's biggest regret was that he could not buy the fair's biggest attractions because Walt Disney kept all of his audio-animatronics. Since Berry also was an owner of the Crescent Park amusement park, it is tantalizing to imagine It's a Small World, President Lincoln or the Carousel of Progress in East Providence.

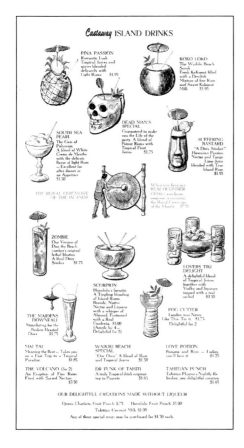

The Copper Galley's drinks menu.
Christopher Scott Martin/Quahog.org.

Berry asked Crescent Park Carousel caretaker Ed Serowik Sr. to carve a huge Tiki figure for the entrance of the Copper Galley, a job that took most of a winter. Ed has no idea of the fate of this carving, which disappeared after the Copper Galley closed, nor of the whereabouts of all those remnants of the World's Fair.

From the Beachcomber Lounge, the Copper Galley or Waikiki Beach, guests could see Gaspee Point where, on June 10, 1772, the British frigate *Gaspee* was burned to protest duties on molasses, an ingredient in rum. The menu reminded drinkers of this, imploring them to strike a blow for freedom by ordering more rum.

Johnson & Wales purchased the Shipyard Marina property and donated the land where the Copper Galley stood to Save the Bay for its headquarters.

TRAPPER JOHN'S

1989–1990
75 Plain Street

Not many people today remember that Buddy Cianci once owned a restaurant in Providence, and a *M*A*S*H*-themed one to boot. Providence mayor Vincent "Buddy" Cianci was briefly involved in the restaurant business in the city—after his first run as mayor, from 1975 to 1984, ended with a felony conviction. In 1989, he opened Trapper John's on Plain Street near Rhode Island Hospital. For a man with such a keen understanding of Providence, he chose a far from downtown location that may have been its downfall, although it was conveniently close to the emergency room.

The Korean War military medic theme was a fun one, and any resemblance to *M*A*S*H* was purely intentional. A military-style ambulance was parked outside, while inside there were army helmet lampshades and camouflage wallpaper. My mother and I stopped in for dinner one winter night, and well, let's just say there was no trouble getting a table. There were two other people there that night, however: the former mayor chatting with a friend in a gorgeous mink coat. He never came over to our table, an odd lapse for a man so known for his sociability and who must have known that he was a bigger draw than the food or the tenuous connection to Hot Lips Houlihan. Dear mother joked that she should have worn her fur. I distinctly remember ordering "Father Mulcahey's Egg Rolls," which were an inventive take with shrimp, pork, mushrooms and bean sprouts, served with honey mustard and wasabi dipping sauces, the latter so unknown at the time that the *Providence Journal* reviewer, Alan Rosenberg, who described the menu as "cutesy/eclectic," felt compelled to explain what wasabi was.

The daily blue plate specials, more than anything, showed Cianci's understanding of his constituents' backgrounds and appetites (Monday: turkey pot pie, Tuesday: lasagna, Wednesday: meatloaf and gravy, Thursday: corned beef and cabbage, Friday: clam cakes and chowder, Saturday: hot turkey sandwich). By 1991, Cianci was back in power as mayor and had bigger things to run than a restaurant, until Operation Plunder Dome led to his resignation in 2002. Even after it closed in 1990, Trapper John's continued to make news, as when a company that had supplied computer systems there moved to attach the mayor's pay or when there was talk of an arson-for-hire scheme involving the property. The Mayor's Own Marinara Sauce, bottled for charity, is the most enduring food legacy for the mayor who called his autobiography *Politics and Pasta.*

FEDERAL RESERVE

1995–1998
Union Trust Building, 60 Dorrance Street

Federal Reserve invested in a double theme to raise interest. First, it capitalized on its location in a former bank in the Union Trust Building to stamp the menu with banking terms, like a wine list titled "liquid assets" and a sandwich called the "George Bailey." There was a secondary theme of Rhode Island food that placed Federal Reserve in the forefront of recognizing and celebrating the Ocean State's unique regional cuisine. The question was whether stuffed quahogs and johnnycakes served in a sumptuous setting of inlaid marble floors, a sixty-foot onyx and Siena marble bar behind which bank tellers once stood and banquettes upholstered in faux leopard would yield dividends.

The brain trust behind Federal Reserve was Bob and Ann Burke of the French restaurant Pot Au Feu. In financing this new project, the Burkes displayed faith in the potential of Providence to regain its luster as an evening destination. This was long before the days when any given night downtown would see thousands of theater and Civic Center patrons vying for parking places and restaurant tables.

One of the first people to dine at Federal Reserve was architecture critic David Brussat, who remembers being served the first J.P. Morgan sandwich ever made for a customer. J.P. stood for jelly and peanut butter. I recall Federal Reserve as a surprisingly affordable and friendly place for a quick but elegant lunch and enjoyed the RISDIC red chowder, named for the Rhode Island Savings and Deposit Indemnity Corporation, awash in red ink at the time. It was a chowder that might have been served at Fields Point a century earlier. I also ordered johnnycakes, since I can never resist them on any menu. Bob Burke is a champ at preparing them and has displayed his technique—frying the cakes made from local white flint corn in bacon grease—on local television.

Even Federal Reserve's signage was banking themed. *Christopher Scott Martin/Quahog.org*

Federal Reserve closed as a restaurant in June 1998, although it continued as a swell venue for private events afterward. It appeared on the scene just before the downtown revival really hit its stride. Nowadays, the Dorrance occupies the former Federal Reserve space, and jaws are still dropping over the cuisine and architecture. Chef Ben Sukle of La Laiterie was the original chef at the Dorrance before he opened his own restaurants Birch and Oberlin. The Dorrance provides a sly Federal Reserve Easter egg with a Baked Alaska Rhody Style, made with coffee milk sorbet.

3
Chinese

CHINATOWN

1903–1914
Empire Street

Many today would be surprised to learn that Providence once had a vibrant Chinatown. To be more precise, it had several of them, although the best known was on Empire Street, before it was widened in 1914. The first Providence Chinatown was located on Burrill Street and apparently contained at least one Chinese restaurant. A friend has shared with me a Chinese restaurant postcard in her collection, postmarked 1901, with the message "This place is on the corner of Burrill and Westminster Street." Unfortunately, the restaurant interior depicted on the card was in fact located in San Francisco. According to Florence Parker Simster in her 1968 book *Streets of the City: An Anecdotal History of Providence*—drawn from her radio program, which began airing in June 1952 on WEAN—at the turn of the century, the building of a theater on Westminster Street (probably the Empire Theater) and the demolition of a tenement house on Chapel Street caused the Chinese to move to Empire Street, which then became the new Chinatown. "All the little buildings which at that time lined Empire Street were taken by the Chinese. Here they sold dried fruits, fish, sausage and unusual sauces," Simster wrote. She also noted that the Chinese drugstore stocked "dried lizards, snakes and powdered reindeer horn." The Benno Wolf block on Empire Street contained the major groceries, business societies and a Masonic lodge. A December 13, 1914 *Providence Sunday Journal* article paints a vivid image: "The front of the block was decorated with fantastic banners, red streamers, peacock feathers and gilt signs, emblazoned with Chinese characters." However, that colorful scene was already doomed because the city decided to demolish the Chinatown buildings so Empire Street could be widened. For the first time, many trudging sadly on foot, a group of people in Providence was moving in its entirety from one part of the city to another. The exodus began in late November 1914, when twenty-five families removed their belonging from their Empire Street homes, prompting a newspaper illustration of four men carrying bundles past a restaurant advertising chop suey. Providence's Chinese inhabitants next moved to Summer Street, where the new Chinatown was housed in one long three-story wooden building.

Chinese restaurants in Providence beyond Chinatown had to contend with several waves of controversy threatening both the manner in which they served their customers and where the popular chop suey places could be located. A "white slavery" panic was set off in 1909 after a nineteen-year-old New York girl, Elsie Sigel, was allegedly murdered by Leon Ling, a waiter at a Chinese restaurant. Sigel's body was found in a trunk in Ling's apartment, and the two had been lovers. Ling disappeared, and the story became sensational tabloid fodder, stoking fears and prejudice in Providence. On June 25, 1909, it was front-page news in the *Providence Journal* when the Providence Police Commission issued an order to Police Chief Patrick Egan to remove the doors and draperies at booths or rooms where food was served at Chinese restaurants in the city. The commission's stated goal, according to the article, was "to keep this class of restaurants as clean and free from suspicion as possible, and the new order means that every booth and stall and room will be open to view at all times." It was clear from the article that the aim was to placate fears that Chinese restaurants were dark and mysterious dens where young women could be seduced. The order for the removal of doors and draperies from booths at Chinese restaurants apparently assured women that Chinese restaurants remained respectable places to eat. The chairman of the Police Commission also condemned the practice of "young white girls taking charge of Chinamen at Sunday Schools," and if male teachers could not be found, he advised that Sunday school should be taught by women of sufficiently advanced age and impeccable character to prevent a repeat of what had occurred in New York. Here, the criticism was likely pointed at Beneficent Church, where many Chinese immigrants worshipped and received instruction in English.

Another challenge to Chinese restaurants in Providence occurred in July 1916. Real estate owners and business people on Westminster Street, over seventy in all, filed a petition with the Board of Police Commissioners requesting that no more licenses be granted for Chinese restaurants on Westminster Street between Market Square and Jackson Street, in the center of the store district in the city's main shopping street. The signers of the petition were connected with most of the large department stores on Westminster Street and complained that additional Chinese restaurants would be detrimental and harmful to their business interests. R.W. Alfred, the secretary and treasurer of the Gladding Dry Goods Company, wrote a letter to the editor of the *Providence Journal*, published on February 4, 1917, on the topic. He wrote, "We believe with many others that there are now enough Chinese restaurants in this city to meet any reasonable demand for such places, and that to allow Westminster Street to be invaded by more restaurants of that kind would be a most serious mistake." He also argued that in Boston Chinese restaurants were not permitted in the main retail district and that more Chinese restaurants would damage the reputation of Westminster Street as a "first-class" business street.

Fortunately, and to the credit of Providence, cooler heads prevailed and this protest was not sustained. A license was granted to Diamond Restaurant Company to open a Chinese restaurant at 230 Westminster Street despite the opposition.

PORT ARTHUR

1921–1965
123 Weybosset Street

Tong Tow (also referred to as "Mr. Tow Fong, Mgr." in the 1927 city directory) and his son He Gong Tow opened the Port Arthur Restaurant in 1921, and it endured until 1965. It was reputed by some to be the first Chinese restaurant in Rhode Island (not true, alas) and heralded itself as the largest Chinese restaurant in New England (possibly). Tong Tow's father came to the United States in 1850 and, after working on the railroads, settled in Pawtucket, where he opened a laundry. The Tows were among the oldest Chinese families in the state.

There was a famous Port Arthur restaurant in New York City, one of that city's first, so the Providence restaurant may have been borrowing some allure by using the same name. Port Arthur (Lushun) was an important port city in China that was frequently in the news at the time, a fact which may also explain the restaurants' names.

Located on Weybosset Street opposite the Narragansett Hotel, Providence's Port Arthur was a glamorous place. A narrow staircase led up to the second-floor dining room. A postcard reveals interiors melding art deco with Chinese influences, a cozy cocktail nook and an expansive dance floor.

Port Arthur advertised that it catered to ladies and gentlemen of exact taste, with dancing daily except Sunday. The entire third floor was an elaborate banquet hall. An alluring marquee for the restaurant dominated Dorrance Street at the corner or Weybosset. Esteemed jazz musician Bobby Hackett (cornet, trumpet and guitar), who later played with Benny Goodman, Glenn Miller and Frank Sinatra, honed his craft playing in a six-piece group, three sessions a day, seven days a week at the Port Arthur in his teens. He was paid

A postcard for Providence's Port Arthur, the largest Chinese restaurant in New England. *Louis McGowan.*

twelve dollars a week. Shoppers at the Outlet across the street were lured into the Port Arthur by the music streaming from open windows. I have seen chopsticks stamped with the Port Arthur name, so they were available, even if most patrons used forks.

During World War II, Port Arthur was perhaps too popular with sailors and soldiers on liberty, because Shore Patrol considered it such a trouble spot that it was nicknamed blood alley. In the postwar years, it became increasingly difficult to fill the block-long dining room, and the Port Arthur closed in 1965. Fortunately, the Tow family's empire of Chinese restaurants continued with the Ming Garden.

MING GARDEN

1942–1987
141 Westminster Street, 66 Exchange Place

Ming Garden was founded in 1942 by Yat K. Tow (1912–1990) with help of his father, Port Arthur's He Gong Tow (1889–1983). Originally called the China Clipper, it was redesigned in the 1950s with a Polynesian theme and a Morris Nathanson–designed Polynesian room and renamed Ming Garden. *Holiday* magazine named it one of the best Chinese restaurants in the country in the 1960s.

Yat K. Tow was the first Chinese American to be inducted into the Rhode Island Heritage Hall of Fame. Tow was born in Canton, China; his mother died when he was six months old, and he was raised by his grandmother before coming to America as a boy. He and his wife, Lilly, made Ming Garden into a fine restaurant with a reputation for a more authentic Chinese menu, the first restaurant in Rhode Island to introduce Mandarin, Szechuan and Hunan cuisine, as well as a meeting place for prominent government and business leaders. Yat's outgoing personality and memory for names and faces helped build a large and devoted following. Yat used his success to provide immigration, education, housing and employment assistance to Providence's Chinese American community. Lilly personally composed and typed advertisements specifically tailored to appeal to many different segments of Providence's population.

There are a few lost Rhode Island foods that people lament loudly and constantly. Among these are the chicken wings from Ming Garden, fondly referred to as Ming Wings. The sauce was black, sticky and shiny, with slivers of garlic. Diners would come to the restaurant just for a few orders of wings, then order them to go and drive them home. One poster on the blog *Art in Ruins* recalls her father, who worked for a jewelry company in Cranston, driving the Ming Wings ten hours home to Virginia. The car would be deliciously perfumed with their aroma for weeks afterward. Ming Wings were for a time available for purchase in local supermarkets, packaged in those familiar Chinese take-out containers with wire handles.

Providence Chinese restaurants always served bread and butter or rolls. The rolls at Ming Garden had a sweet pork mixture in the middle. A fan recalls a bartender named Leo who made great whiskey sours and remembered everyone's favorite drink.

Ming Garden had entrances on both Westminster Street, leading to the bar, and Exchange Place, opening into the downstairs Chrysanthemum dining room. Ming Garden had the reputation of being a bit more elegant than other Chinese restaurants, with starched linens, the upstairs Persimmon Room in particular.

When He Gong Charles Tow died in June 1983 at the age of ninety-four, he had earned a reputation as the father of Chinese restaurants in Rhode Island. Until a few days before his death, he worked at the Ming Garden.

A 1986 renovation resulted in a name change to simply "The Ming" and the introduction of new Chinese dishes featuring clay pot cooking as well as a kosher-style deli. In late 1987, the Ming closed, citing increasing competition downtown.

LUKE'S CHINESE AMERICAN RESTAURANT

1951–1990
59 Eddy Street

Just behind city hall, Luke's restaurant was opened by Tin Cheung Luke and his son Henry in 1951 in the basement and first-floor space once occupied by the opulent Rathskeller and, from the early 1930s to mid-1940s, by the French restaurant Old France. The restaurant was on the first floor, and an old postcard reveals a homey space with a stone fireplace and wood paneling that could have dated from the Rathskeller days. A small television sits on top of the fireplace mantel.

... REAR OF CITY HALL, PROVIDENCE, R. I.

A postcard reveals the cozy knotty pine–paneled interior of Luke's Chinese American restaurant. *Louis McGowan.*

The dishes people still pine for from Luke's are the beef fried rice and pupu platters with skewers of beef you could cook over an open flame. In the mid-60s, my aunt and uncle fell in love in a red vinyl booth at Luke's, over veal with brown gravy served in a silver platter, the cover dramatically lifted and releasing steam into the dimly lit atmosphere. The lobster Cantonese in lobster sauce or filet mignon in oyster sauce were the dishes to order if you were in the mood for a splurge. The chefs made real duck sauce, not the plastic packet stuff.

The Luau Hut, decorated with straw matting and featuring round-back rattan chairs, was in the basement (site of the former ladies' restaurant of the Rathskeller). The cocktail menu featured amusingly named potations, served in coconuts, pineapples and special glasses featuring hula dancers and idols. There were suggestions based on your mood and romantic inclinations. There was the Coco Kow (fresh coconut, sweet cream and assorted rums), the Surf Rider ("daring and exciting as skimming over the crest of the wave"), Wahine's Delight ("soft and graceful as a Tahitian dancer"), Witches Brew ("The wrath of a woman scorned. Guaranteed to mend a broken heart"), the South Pacific ("For rebels of all ages sure to cement the union"), Devil's Gold ("Give the Devil his due—this is a delicious, beautiful gold drink"), Rum Cow ("Potent elixir with amazing powers") and the Pina Paradise ("A favorite in the islands. A fresh pineapple filled with a subtle concoction. Appealing to the eye and delightful to the taste"). Servers recall that carrying food downstairs from the kitchen to the Luau Hut was perilous because the stairs could become greasy as the night went on.

Henry Luke sold the restaurant in 1978, although it continued to operate under the Luke's name until the early '90s. Henry, who died in 1991, later owned the King's Inn restaurant in Cumberland. In the 1980s, Luke's attempted to attract a younger clientele. A 1981 ad in the Providence College newspaper the *Cowl* invited students to "Try Chinese Food Downtown" and promised the ultimate in Polynesian, Chinese and American fare. "Our exotic tropical drinks are served in a relaxing, secluded island atmosphere," the ad continued. Nowadays, trying Chinese food downtown is all but impossible, an astonishing development for a city in which not even the demolition of Chinatown and the opposition of the biggest merchants in the city could impede the growth and success of its Chinese restaurants.

A photo of owner T. Cheung Luke was featured in an advertisement for Luke's. *Christopher Scott Martin/Quahog.org*

MEE HONG

1938–1979
102 Westminster Street

The Chin family opened Mee Hong in 1938 in a prominent location on Westminster Street to the left of the historic Arcade. The chef Fook "Sarge" Chin had been a cook in the U.S. Army and was just as adept at cooking American fare as Chinese.

The grand opening announcement for Mee Hong proclaimed that the restaurant served excellent American and Chinese food, with a businessmen's luncheon served all day for thirty cents, including a vegetable, a potato and tea or coffee. The roast chicken dinner cost forty-five cents, and there was a full-course Sunday dinner (Sundays were quiet downtown) available for only forty cents. As for the Chinese food, Mee Hong assured prospective customers that the restaurant would serve "Real Chinese Dishes Boston China-Town Style." Of course, Providence had lost its own Chinatown by then. The Chinese dishes included chicken chow mein, chicken chop suey, fried rice, subgum chow men and "egg foo yong."

The green tables were custom-designed for the restaurant and had the letters *M* and *H* drawn in the center. The plates were decorated with hummingbirds. The restaurant did not have a liquor license. Mee Hong meals came with French bread and side dishes of coleslaw, oversized pickled beets, peas and long length-of-a-potato french fries. The fries had a pleasingly soft texture. It was a place where you could order chow mein, chop suey or an open-faced hot turkey sandwich. Veal cutlet with brown gravy was a popular menu item, and Mee Hong could also be relied on for a huge piece of batter-fried fish and chips as well. An inexpensive item on the menu, popular with the lunch crowd of businessmen and women, was the chow mein sandwich (chow mein and noodles served over a hamburger bun). There was a large, circular red neon sign over the doorway. A brass plate near the front door beckoned with the lovely words, "Through these doors pass the nicest people we know." After the restaurant closed, the building was demolished for a parking lot.

The Chin family also converted a diner in East Providence into a Chinese restaurant called the China Star, more commonly known as the "China Dinah."

4
Diners and Lunches

SILVER TOP DINER

1938–2002
13 Harris Avenue

The Silver Top was perhaps the best-known diner in Providence. Food writers Jane and Michael Stern called it a fascinating mix of "club hoppers and insomniacs." They were not the only the writers to bring the Silver Top to the notice of a national audience. In 1980, even *The Official Preppy Handbook* singled out the Silver Top Diner as a place in Providence where the preps hang out. It certainly attracted the best, the brightest and the hungriest. Louis Armstrong wandered in one night.

Originally owned and operated by Leo Katz and his family, the Silver Top's first structure was wood, before the diner manufactured by Kullman Dining Car Company of Harrison, New Jersey, was moved to the site. The presence of the produce warehouse nearby guaranteed both hungry truck drivers, who started arriving at the produce landing with their deliveries of cases of cauliflower, peppers and cantaloupes at 2:00 a.m., and the constant availability of fresh fruit and vegetables. The Katz family owned the diner for about thirty years. From around 1965 to 1980, it was owned by Dorothy and Anthony Laddish. Around 1980, the diner was purchased by Mabel Selvage, who had moved to Rhode Island from New Jersey, and she added her name (sort of) to the historic place.

Providence's renaissance did not include a place for its most famous diner, the Silver Top. *Christopher Scott Martin/Quahog.org.*

Many people still remember it as Joann's Silver Top. Apparently, Mabel's husband did not like her given name, so she called herself and her diner Joann's. However, it was really supposed to be spelled Jo-Ann on the sign, but the sign maker forgot the hyphen. That is the story of how Joann's Silver Top came to be and of why the owner and cook people remember as Joann was really named Mabel.

The Joann's Silver Top Diner sign that was placed on the roof by Selvage in 1980 was derided by diner purists, especially in contrast to the original signs for "vaculator coffee" and "infra-red broiling" on either side of the words "air conditioned" on the cornice. No one was too upset when that Joann's sign disappeared.

An old matchbook for the diner plugged the coffee, on which the fortunes of any diner rose and fell. "Fresh coffee is delicious at the Silver Top. Because our coffee is brewed every 20 minutes, or less, you will always enjoy a FRESH cup of coffee at any hour of the day or night." In the first part of its history, the diner was open twenty-four hours and had little difficulty in keeping the six booths and seventeen counter stools filled.

Another matchbook, from the 1960s, repeated the promise that the coffee was brewed every twenty minutes and added further reassurances that the Silver Top had been "enjoying public confidence for over 25 years" and served "wholesome food" in an atmosphere of "sparkling cleanliness."

Mabel always said that the most popular item on the menu was the coffee and the second-most popular was a refill. However, the food also had its passionate adherents. Popular dishes were Thursday's special of New England boiled dinner, the red chowder on Fridays, the blueberry pancakes and grilled muffins. Personally helming the grill, Mabel cooked the eggs on the left and potatoes for the home fries, served sprinkled with granulated garlic, on the right.

During Mabel's tenure, the diner served only late at night and early morning, opening at midnight and closing at 10:00 a.m. Keeping those hours was not without some risk. In February 1984, a masked man with a sawed-off shotgun robbed the diner's register of $125 at 2:30 a.m. and also took $60 from Mabel herself after ordering her and the patrons onto the floor. Thankfully, no one was injured—except perhaps the already battered reputation of diners.

The jukebox was well curated and popular. Local singer and songwriter Billy Mitchell recorded a tune called "The Diva of the Silver Top Diner" about a fictional "superstar of the breakfast bar" with a voice like an angel, but there is no indication that Mabel ever sang.

The Silver Top was driven on Route 95 to Pawtucket on March 12, 2002.
Christopher Scott Martin/Quahog.org.

In 1984, Mabel was paying all of $171.67 in monthly rent for the lot on which the Silver Top stood. The land had originally been owned by the city but was later transferred to the Providence Redevelopment Agency, which had grander visions for it than a diner serving good cheap coffee to the city's working people. One effect of the renaissance of Providence was that the tax-generating revenue of places like the Silver Top Diner was miniscule compared to the development potential of the land under and around them. Providence was on its way up again, and the Silver Top's days were numbered. Mabel herself was looking forward to retirement in West Virginia. Several other owners kept the Silver Top going for another fourteen years, most notably Pat Brown, who passionately defended its right to remain in the city. The Silver Top was driven, quite literally, out of Providence on March 12, 2002, just before 9:00 a.m., after it had been lifted from its location onto a flatbed truck.

Plans by Brown to reopen the Silver Top in Pawtucket fell through. It was reported that neighbors of the proposed new site there were opposed to an all-night diner. The diner building has since been bought by Katie Cerrone, who serves excellent burgers and nostalgia at her KC Burger Bars. Home-baked pies and foot-long hotdogs may yet be served in the old Kullman with the silver top.

KOERNER'S LUNCH

1929–1983
44 Aborn Street, 33 Broadway and 18 Aborn Street

Frank Koerner was as much of a saint as can be found in the annals of Providence restaurant history. While he and his lunchroom (located first at 44 Aborn Street and later at 33 Broadway) may not have been responsible for any miracles, there are many examples of his goodness, described by *Providence Journal* reporter Philip C. Gunion in October 1959, when Koerner was retiring.

He opened his restaurant at 5:00 a.m. and would often find a line of at least fifteen homeless men out front. That is why he arrived even earlier on cold days, so he could let them into the warmth while he started the coffee.

Those who lived on pensions received one check a month, on the first, and often ran out of money weeks before the next check arrived. Frank extended credit to them so they could continue to eat at Koerner's. He was patient about repayment, and yet, when he retired, there were only six unpaid accounts.

He served a Rhode Island specialty that has all but disappeared from local menus in these more prosperous times, kidney beans with toast (or roll and butter). This dish provided the calories to keep on living for many people during hard times. As late as 1959, he only charged fifteen cents for kidney beans with toast.

Koerner fed prisoners being held at Providence police headquarters overnight. He also kept the police and fire departments nourished, often taking in about forty dollars a day (at a time when a full dinner cost sixty cents) from takeout meals ordered by personnel from the nearby police and fire headquarters.

From 1929 to 1953, Koerner's Lunch served about 1,200 people a day. During the World War II years alone, when records had to be kept for rationing purposes, Koerner served over 3 million people. The menu was Spartan. The nickel cup of coffee was a big draw. For breakfast, a quarter bought a bowl of oatmeal served with a muffin and coffee. A pint bottle of milk with cereal cost fifteen cents. Pea soup and crackers was a lunch favorite for fifteen cents.

Before opening his own lunchroom in 1929, which he ran for thirty years, Koerner had already worked for twenty-five years at Brooks Beanery on Washington Street. Thus, for fifty-five years, he worked a shift of 5:00 a.m. to 3:30 p.m., which entailed getting up at 1:30 in the morning, since he liked a few hours to himself first.

Koerner was born in Willimantic, Connecticut, but moved to Rhode Island when he was only two. When he began his restaurant career in 1904, workers like him did not get a day off and were paid $10.50 per week for eighty-four hours of work. By 1914, however, he was earning $14 per week, a raise from $0.13 cents to $0.17 per hour.

Upon his retirement at age seventy-three, Koerner hoped to spend time in Florida and to take up fishing and bowling. Koerner's Lunch continued under the ownership of brothers John and Louis Katsetos, who moved the business to its final location at 18 Aborn Street. Louis Katsetos cooked everything from scratch and loved to feed people, just as Frank Koerner had. The clientele never really changed, nor did people's need for the nourishment and respect Koerner's provided. Louis lived in Cathedral Square, around the corner from the restaurant, and walked to work, opening Koerner's at 6:00 a.m. and closing at 7:00 p.m.

Benjamin Philbrick's 1970 film *Koerners, A Lunch* captures a morning at Koerner's. A hunched man walks to the counter to return a borrowed newspaper. Signs for Virginia ham, chicken pie and muffins come into view. The enamel-topped tables and bentwood chairs look like they date back to 1929. Louis Katsetos, in a short-sleeved white shirt and black tie, busies himself around the restaurant. He hangs signs for the daily specials in the window, pours something, maybe cereal, into a bowl and shakes a customer's hand. Men wear hats. The final frame is an old sign reading "Koerner's Lunch Home Cooking/Good Eating Place/Ladies Invited."

Koerner's closed in 1983, ordered to vacate 18 Aborn Street and unable to find an affordable location elsewhere. Louis might have closed earlier but hoped, mistakenly as it turned out, that the new Federal Building on Westminster Street would drum up business. Koerner's had always appealed to the really hungry rather than the well-heeled lunch crowd. Koerner's did not get the miracle it so justly deserved.

MIKE'S WAGON

1916 (possibly earlier)–1991
Various Locations

Providence is credited as the birthplace of the diner, the American institution that developed from horse-drawn "lunch wagons" that fed the night shift when other restaurants in the city were closed. By the 1920s, many of these wagons, expanded with interior seating and clever adornment adapted to their diminutive size, settled into permanent locations and became known as diners. However, two mobile lunch wagons persisted well past the others, although they were later moved by horseless conveyances. The most famous of these is Haven Brothers, still serving hot dogs and hangover-preventing fried egg–topped murder burgers to the night leisure crowd. But Mike's Wagon was once just as much a fixture in Providence by night as Haven Brothers.

It is hard to say exactly when Mike's Wagon started serving downtown, but a license was issued to Thomas E. Lynch for its operation in 1916. The original location was Francis Street, and it set up around 5:30 p.m. serving until dawn. The menu at Mike's consisted of coffee, hamburgers, hot dogs, chili, steak sandwiches, egg salad and chicken salad.

In 1943, Mike's was granted a permanent spot with a water hookup to be able to make coffee. Since it was wartime, the decision appeared to make sense, as gasoline and tires to move the wagon twice a day would be spared for other purposes in that time of scarcity. However, tongues wagged that Mike's Wagon's attorney was Thomas Roberts, the brother of then mayor Dennis J. Roberts. Opposition rallied against the wagon in what sounds like one of the most contentious water hookups in history. Apparently, Mike's was not being charged for the water. In its defense, Mike's attorney argued that the water was only used for coffee because Mike's did not serve drinking water. The decision was later reversed based on the results of a traffic study (yes, they had those then too) finding that the twenty-four-hour presence of the wagon would disrupt daytime traffic. Some people were not happy that the Ever Ready Diner, then located on Charles Street, also had a hookup to the city water (and sewer) and were not keen to see further exceptions like that. To those who did not yet prize diners and lunch wagons as institutions to treasure, Mike's was tolerable, barely, as a nighttime Barnum and Bailey world best gone from the city by early morning.

In November 1965, Mike's Wagon fell on its front end when a coupling pin broke as a tractor was wheeling it into its night location, across from the Biltmore at the time. The customer stools, food and plates all fell onto the street as the impact of the front of the diner hitting the ground after it decoupled snapped the front part of the diner away. A photo depicts perplexed cook and waiter John Ramsey posing in the open maw of the wagon, but he was standing on the street when the smash happened. The accident occurred at 6:00 p.m., when it was about to open, and fortunately there were no customers in the wagon at the time. Owner Michael D'Antuono could not put a dollar amount to the damage to the yellow-and-blue diner wagon.

Mike's operated on West Exchange Street, behind the Civic Center, from 1983 to 1991, when it lost its spot to the new Providence Convention Center. Its hours there were 5:00 p.m. to 3:00 a.m. It then moved to Dyer Market on Valley Street while petitioning the city for a new location on Exchange Terrance near Kennedy Plaza. However, in a battle which was cast as poor little diner (twenty-six feet long and ten feet wide, with twelve stools and a countertop) versus rich corporation, Mike's Wagon lost. Cookson America had redeveloped the old train station as office and restaurant space and opposed having Mike's as a neighbor because it would block views of the park and create litter.

A long-running feud between two employees led one to burn down the house of the other. In a separate incident, one of the co-owners was murdered. Stories like these in the local paper did not help the diner's case.

As one of Providence's two remaining mobile diners, Mike's was not able to rally the same support as Haven Brothers, but its history was nearly as long and certainly colorful. The diner turned up for sale on eBay in 2011.

ARMAND'S

1950s–1980
358 Westminster Street

Nothing can bring a lost restaurant to life like its menu. It is dispiriting how few menus remain for the places discussed in this book. In the case of Armand's, if Christine Francis of Carmen & Ginger Vintage Goods in the Arcade had not unearthed a menu, I may not have included it. But what a menu, quixotic spellings and all, and what a find of a lost restaurant.

The menu cover lures diners with a mélange of cuisine, from the German American vein ("Frankforts and Potato Salad") to delicatessen ("1/4 lb. Hot Corned Beef or Pastromi on Jewish Rye") to what the place really did best, classic Italian American cooking ("Meat Balls and Spaghetti" and "Breaded Veal Cutlet with Spaghetti"). Armand's promised that is was comfortably air conditioned for those who chose to dine in, but orders were also "put up to take out" and could be delivered.

The second page of the menu offers an "only in Rhode Island" hasty lunch of two johnnycakes with pork sausages, home fries, apple sauce and butter for sixty cents. The hamburgers are remembered by at least one person I spoke to on a Providence walking tour, and there is even a fried pepper–topped "pepperburger."

The Italian menu at Armand's is similar to what can be found at many of the most popular Italian restaurants around the state today, and this fare has become the predominant cuisine of the state after its local seafood. Armand's had baked stuffed lasagna (Thursdays only), eggplant "parmeggiana" en casserole, homemade ravioli with meat sauce, Italian antipasto or Italian sausage or meatball sandwiches served on a torpedo roll. The meatball sandwich could be topped with fried peppers or uniquely soffritto (Armand's called it "Soffirtto," which may have been a localism or a misspelling). In any

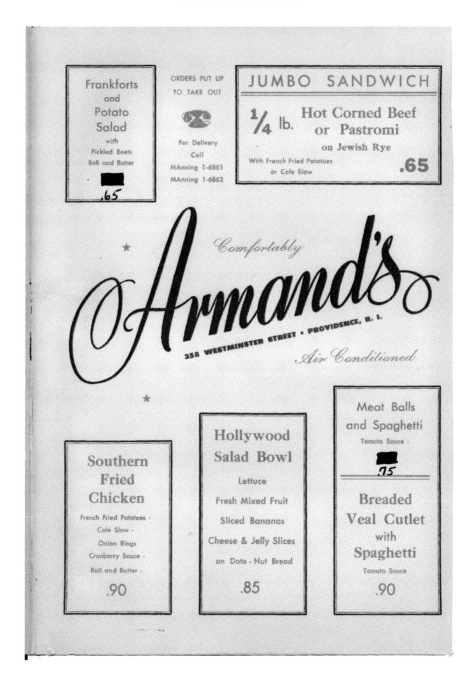

Armand's menu reveals some handwritten price increases. *Christine Francis/Carmen & Ginger.*

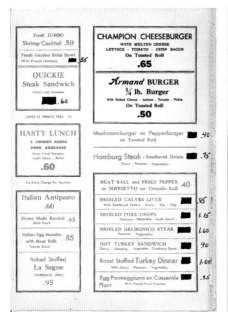

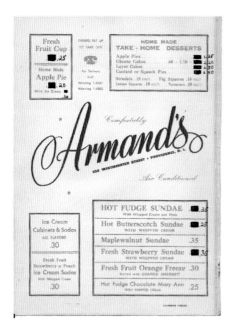

Armand's had everything from johnnycakes to lasagna on the menu. There were many fried seafood choices, and Armand's dessert choices included cabinets (the Rhode Island term for milkshakes). *Christine Francis/ Carmen & Ginger.*

case, topping a meatball sandwich with diced and sautéed onion, carrot and celery is a brilliant idea contemporary restaurants should emulate.

Dieters could feel good about ordering the Hollywood Salad Bowl, of lettuce, mixed fresh fruit and sliced bananas served with a side of cream cheese and jelly on date nut bread. If I had a nickel for every piece of date nut bread sold at the lost restaurants of Providence… Date nut bread, like Bing Crosby, does not seem to have withstood the test of time.

Of course, this being Providence, Armand's also offered fried clams, scallops or sole every night, as well as New England–style fish and chips on Fridays. Hot turkey sandwiches and roast stuffed turkey dinner rounded out the menu, which concluded with ice cream cabinets, sundaes or homemade apple pie. *Cabinet* is the local term for milkshakes or frappes.

A similar formula (chicken, eggplant and meatball Parmesan, turkey sandwiches, clams casino) has been reimagined by Major Food Group's Parm in New York City's Little Italy to amazing success and long lines. Major Food Group has recently even taken over the old space of New York's Four Seasons restaurant.

Armand's undoubtedly benefitted from its location close by the RKO Albee Theater, department stores and the downtown business district, and one local woman reminisced about eating there after ballet class.

EDDIE & SON

1944–2013
74 Dorrance Street

There was nothing fancy about Eddie & Son. The specials were written on paper plates taped to the windows. The cheese melted over the eggplant, veal and chicken was American, not Parmesan, but the sauce was long simmered with meatballs and sausage. It was only open until 3:00 p.m. and was small and crowded with about fifty seats.

Eddie & Son started in 1944 at the corner of Broadway and Federal and was called the Sherbrook initially. In 1949, it moved to the corner of Pine and Dorrance and was known there simply as Eddie's. Here, Eddie's had to contend with flooding from Hurricane Carol and closed for a month. In 1959, Eddie's moved to Westminster Street but was displaced in 1982 when the Fleet Center was built. From there, this most peripatetic of lost restaurants moved to a basement location at 127 Dorrance Street with eighty-five seats, close to the Garrahy courthouse, making it very popular with lawyers, judges and court employees. After twelve years there, Eddie's moved to its last location at 74 Dorrance Street in 1994.

Eddie was Edward Caputo and Tom Caputo was the Son, who worked at the restaurant from the age of eleven. Eddie also was a musician who played with the Rhode Island Philharmonic. After Eddie retired in 1975, Tom and his wife, Connie, took over, with Connie managing the front of the house. I only knew the final location, where I experienced the lightning-fast service (some called it Fast Eddie's) and the cash only policy. I developed an unfortunate addiction to the meatball, peppers and fries plate. The baked stuffed eggplant was also wrapped around those meatballs and baked with layers of American cheese.

Eddie & Son closed on Friday, August 23, 2013, as popular as ever, but its owners had decided it was time to take life a little easier. After all, Tom and Connie were well past retirement age and the next generation of the family had pursued other careers.

Diners miss the three-egg omelettes, the bacon cheeseburgers, the chicken parm and the baked rigatoni pasta. The escarole soup had fans too. No one else seems to miss the American cheese, but to me it was what made Eddie's so comforting and enticing, and I often wonder why other Italian American chefs have not caught on that nothing else melts so nicely.

McGARRY'S

1953–1985
The Howard Building

McGarry's occupied a prime downtown location on Exchange Place (later Kennedy Plaza), diagonally across from city hall, in the spot formerly occupied by the venerable Gibson's. In fact, it was a successor to Gibson's, with a similar menu of sandwiches, flavorful sundaes and fountain refreshments. Gibson's was bought by John P. "Bud" McGarry with his father and brothers in 1953 and renamed McGarry's. He also owned McGarry's 1025 Club in Johnston. This change of hands occurred, unfortunately, just before Hurricane Carol in 1954 caused severe damage to the foundation of the Howard Building, which had already been

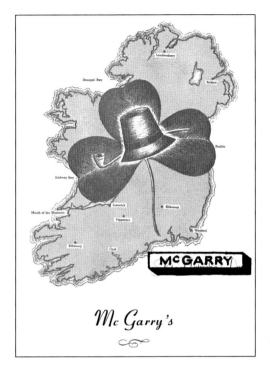

A McGarry's menu from the 1960s.
Christine Francis/Carmen & Ginger.

undermined by the 1938 hurricane and finally had to be torn down in 1957. In 1960, McGarry's moved into the new Howard Building.

There was overlap in personnel between Gibson's and McGarry's. Jane Phillips worked as a waitress at Gibson's and later McGarry's for forty-three years in all, and her retirement party in June 1985 brought out many of her regulars to say goodbye. During World War II, she started working at Gibson's in order to pay her bills, and she piquantly recalled service members coming to the restaurant for Thanksgiving and Christmas and, with nowhere else to go, arriving in the morning, feeding the jukebox and staying all day. Jane estimated that 70 percent of her McGarry's customers came in every day and the other 30 percent came in two to three times a week.

Some came to McGarry's after shopping, others for lunch with grandmother, but most used it as an adjunct waiting room for the buses, which stopped just outside the big plate-glass windows. As long as they spent a quarter, patrons could sit in comfort at a booth. The hamburger in a red plastic basket is fondly remembered by many people I have spoken to about this favorite lost restaurant. It was billed just that way ("Hamburger in Basket") on the menu, which described the burger as served open style on a golden-brown toasted roll, with "French Fried" potatoes and pickle slices for

Left: The hamburger in a basket was the most popular menu choice at McGarry's. *Christine Francis/Carmen & Ginger.*

Right: McGarry's menu warned there was a minimum charge of twenty-five cents per person for booth service. *Christine Francis/Carmen & Ginger.*

forty-nine cents. The pricier seventy-five-cent mushroom burger, served with mushroom gravy, also had its passionate adherents. The menu offered a hot turkey sandwich with brown gravy, cranberry sauce, potato and vegetable for a dollar, a dish that was once ubiquitous at local restaurants. That brown gravy was excellent over french fries.

The McGarry's menu offers some clues that it is a Rhode Island establishment, like the seafood options of fried scallops, fried sole and lobster salad, as well as cabinets (all flavors) and malted milk cabinets.

For a time in the 1960s, McGarry's had a second location at 222 Westminster Street, at the corner of Eddy Street. By the time it closed for good in 1985, with nary a notice, McGarry's/Gibson's had witnessed the city's rise, fall, two world wars, two major hurricanes and the start of Providence's renaissance. Today, there is a 7-Eleven in what was once the best restaurant location in Providence.

CENTRAL LUNCH (PIE ALLEY)

1916–1953
95 Clemence Street

The house specialty at Central Lunch was the five-cent wedge of homemade pie. The pie was so good that narrow Clemence Street came to be known as Pie Alley and the owner George Bellegris nicknamed "Pie Alley George." Central Lunch opened in 1916, a time when quick lunches served across a counter were gaining favor over more traditional and heavy midday fare. But that did not mean you could not enjoy a large piece of pie with the noon meal.

George Bellegris was born in Asopos, Greece, in 1881 and arrived in Providence in 1907. A founder of the Annunciation Greek Orthodox Church of Greater Providence, George served on the building committee of the church's first building at 265 Pine Street, erected in 1922. One can only speculate on what kinds of pies were served by George and his wife, Violet, at Pie Alley, although they were likely the apple, squash and custard pies popular in Providence at that time. The couple had other successful business interests (they purchased Wightman's Diner in South Attleboro, Massachusetts, a poolroom on Ocean Road in Narragansett and the Sea Ranch beach in Jerusalem), but it all started with a pie. All those nickels spent at Pie Alley in Providence helped fund a schoolhouse in George's village in Greece, and during World War II, George shipped livestock, food and clothing to Asopos.

Other businesses located nearby in Pie Alley were Harry's Delicatessen, Victory Bar, Colangelo Domenico Pool Room and the New York Shoe Repairing Company. When Mirabar was located at 93 Clemence Street in the 1960s, the block took on a secondary patina of history and was known as Gay Alley. George sold Central Lunch in 1953 and died in 1972. The building has since been demolished, and there is no more alley, pie or otherwise.

EAST SIDE DINER

1945–1980
360 Waterman Street (Near Red Bridge)

The East Side Diner was owned by Nicholas Ricamo and his wife, Dorothy O'Brien Ricamo, for thirty-five years before they retired in 1980. Nicholas served with the Providence Police Department from 1936 to 1946. The East Side Diner was known especially for its steak sandwiches and show-stopping whipped cream pies, a combination that still drives business at popular local chains Chelo's and Gregg's today. The Rhode Island steak sandwich is, by the way, perhaps the least talked about of iconic local dishes. It is a thin whole grilled rib eye, served on a grilled and buttered torpedo roll, sometimes topped with melted American cheese, onions and mushrooms. A grilled ham, Cheddar and sweet onion sandwich pressed in a cast-iron sandwich press was another popular selection at the East Side Diner. Nicholas Ricamo's banana cream pie had seven bananas in each one.

Buddy Cianci knew he would win his first election as mayor of Providence in 1974 when he walked into the East Side Diner the week before the election and everyone in the restaurant stood and clapped. If he had the East Side, he had the city.

My grandmother Helen Stone worked nights in a very interesting position at the East Side Diner. She was a verifier. She described her duties as ensuring that the food that left the kitchen matched what was written on the checks. This was to prevent servers from inflating their tips by smuggling out free extra food to their favorite customers. Whether the "verifier" was a common position in old diners or one particular to this place run by a former police officer, I have not been able to determine. My grandmother's gentleman friend Mel, himself a former state trooper, was a cook at the East Side Diner and even in retirement in Florida was cooking old recipes from the restaurant, like the Grapenut and rice puddings.

The East Side Diner (by then it was also known as the East Side Restaurant) closed in 1980. Business had never really been the same since the old Red Bridge, connecting Waterman Street to East Providence over the Seekonk River and bringing so much traffic past the diner's doors, closed in 1969.

Nicholas Ricamo later made pies and cakes for Frankie's, owned by his brother in Seekonk, and his desserts were still a huge draw. He passed away in 1988.

After Ricamo retired, the East Side Diner did not stay empty. Jimmy Roccio moved his diner there from Washington Street, renaming it as Jimmy's East Side. A restaurant called Humphrey's was scheduled to open there when a fire that had apparently been set destroyed the old diner in 1982.

EVER READY DINER

1930s–1984
50 Admiral Street

Ah, those great old self-descriptive names of diners. Open twenty-four hours a day, the Ever Ready truly lived up to the name. Its owners boasted that it only closed once, on August 11, 1945, the day Japan surrendered, and even then it was only because they ran out of food. Operated continuously by the Conley and Heffernan families, the Ever Ready was originally a lunch cart in the middle of Charles Street. It was controversial in the city that it was allowed a permanent water and sewer hookup.

The Ever Ready Diner on display at the Johnson & Wales Culinary Museum. *Christopher Scott Martin/Quahog.org.*

The interior of the Ever Ready Diner. *Christopher Scott Martin/Quahog.org.*

That first establishment was demolished to make way for Route 146, a highway between Providence and Worcester. The new Ever Ready then opened in 1958 on Admiral Street in a refurbished diner built by the Worcester Lunch Car Company. The Ever Ready was especially popular with truck driver regulars who appreciated being greeted by name.

Everyone loved the hot dogs. Boiled and served on toasted rolls, these were tender-skinned franks made by Meinel Brothers in Olneyville. They tasted best washed down with coffee milk.

The location of the Ever Ready alongside Route 146 accounted for perhaps its greatest moment, when it became a place of refuge during the blizzard of 1978. Hundreds of stranded drivers who had to abandon their snowed-in cars took shelter in the first open and warm establishment they could find. The old reliable Ever Ready with its piping hot coffee was the first responder. There were so many people gathered in or around the Ever Ready that the state police knew something had to be done. They evacuated the crowd to a police building nearby.

In 1984, the Ever Ready closed, like many lost restaurants, because its owners were ready to move on. By that point, Meinel Brothers had also stopped making its special hot dogs.

The Ever Ready became one of the first exhibits at the Johnson & Wales Culinary Museum, moved there intact. Unfortunately, plans to operate it at the museum as a working diner did not come to pass and the only chef in it is a mannequin, and he won't remember your name.

5

Chains

CHILDS RESTAURANT

1900–1974
142 Westminster Street

The Childs chain of restaurants was started by the Childs brothers in 1889, and by the end of the nineteenth century it had rapidly expanded. By the 1930s, there were over one hundred Childs restaurants in the United States and Canada. One of the secrets to the success of Childs was that it projected an image of modernity and cleanliness with white uniforms and glazed white tiles, walls and tabletops, and in fact, its owners were obsessive about hygiene. Architecture critic Lewis Mumford prized Childs for its neatness, chastity and "antiseptic elegance." Its restaurants had a consistent look from city to city.

The Providence Childs was originally Wolfe's Dairy Lunch Room and was owned by Henry Stewart Wolfe, a former Childs manager. Wolfe was born in New Jersey in 1869 and moved to New York City in 1895 to work for Childs Restaurants. He quickly became a manager and specialized in opening new restaurants for the chain. The location Wolfe selected for his own restaurant was carefully chosen. Most of Providence's streetcar lines passed by its location in the Lauderdale Building with the alluring word *Oysters* over the front door and a porcelain lettered sign promising "sterling coffee."

A postcard for Wolfe's from around 1900. *Louis McGowan.*

Wolfe's was almost opposite the Butler Exchange and the avenue to Union Station. An association with Childs was a major selling point, and the window also announced that Wolfe was "formerly with Childs N.Y. City." Men sat in the front of the restaurant at plain tables of six, while there was a more formal reserved section in the back with tablecloths for women and families, where waitresses in white shirts and black below-the-ankle skirts assured propriety. Around 1910, Wolfe's made the transformation to a Childs Restaurant, renovated to the chain's gleaming standards.

The heyday of Childs in Providence was the 1920s, when downtown was a nighttime destination. Its location on Westminster Street, just to the right of the Arcade, was a perfect site for catering to workers in the surrounding buildings and easily accessible on brightly lit streets from the downtown theaters and College Hill. It stayed open all night to take advantage of the late theater, nightclub and post-dance college crowds. Like other places that never closed, Childs took on an entirely different character depending on the time of day. Popular with office workers during the day, it provided sanctuary for the demimonde in the wee hours. Thirteen waitresses worked until 3:00 a.m. to feed the crowds.

In the front window, in a brilliant stroke of food theater, a chef in a tall white hat made griddle cakes and butter cakes. Butter cakes were like

Childs restaurant was located just past the Arcade. A sign out front says, "Cars stop here." *Providence Public Library.*

an English muffin and could be ordered toasted, split down the middle and browned to crispy perfection. Lyrics from the Comden and Green and Leonard Bernstein musical *Wonderful Town* about a classically trained actress reduced to flipping flapjacks at Childs confirm that women as well as men worked as window griddle cooks and the job may have been an audition for bigger things.

Walter Crocker was the griddle chef at the Providence Childs in the 1920s and later shared the recipe for butter cakes with a nostalgic reporter. Both the batter for the pancakes and the dough for the butter cakes were made from scratch. The pancakes got a rise from something called matzoon, a Bulgarian yeast. Walter Crocker remained a manager for Childs until it closed in 1974.

Sometime during the '30s, the hygienic white tiles were covered with plaster and linoleum. Childs cut its hours during the war years because of a shortage of workers. By the 1960s, it closed at 9:00 p.m. Providence no longer had a late-night crowd. If only it could have held on until WaterFire.

WALDORF LUNCH

1904–1970
10 and 364 Westminster Street and 40 Dorrance Street

Waldorf Lunch was a New England–based chain, founded in 1904 in Springfield, Massachusetts, by Henry Kelsey. By 1929, there were 147 Waldorf locations serving fifty-two million meals a year. The Waldorf System relied on a central commissary in a city like Providence to prepare food for multiple lunchrooms. There were two locations on Westminster Street alone. The profit margin was small, about two and a half cents per meal served in 1921. An advertising motto around that time was "There'll be good, fresh coffee at the Waldorf today. It's always the same." The Dutch name *Waldorf* ("wooded village") was purportedly chosen for its reassuring and refreshing associations with Dutch housekeeping rather than to trade on the fame of the New York hotel. Each Waldorf Lunch was inspected four times a day, and the company touted that it used 398,000 pounds of cleaning powder annually. Waldorf System restaurants were initially concentrated in Providence, Pawtucket, Boston, Springfield, Hartford, New Haven, Rochester and Buffalo. The biggest sellers were coffee, pie, baked beans and ham sandwiches. Despite the attention to cleanliness, there were a few unfortunate legal cases in Providence, arising from complaints of a piece of wood in the baked beans and a chicken bone in the chicken soup. To call them lunches was a bit of a misnomer since many were open twenty-four hours. A pair of notable night owls dined together at a Providence Waldorf Lunch.

H.P. Lovecraft, the world's foremost author of weird fiction, and Harry Houdini, the greatest magician in history, dined together at the Waldorf Lunch in Providence after Houdini's show in September 1926. If only Houdini had left us a trick for traveling back in time to eavesdrop on what they discussed and, more importantly for the purposes of this book, what they ate. Fortunately, there was someone else present at that table who left a record, Muriel Eddy.

There is no better guide to Lovecraft's eating habits in Providence that his friend Muriel E. Eddy. Muriel recorded her memories of Lovecraft in her book *The Gentleman from Angell Street*, co-written with her husband, C.M. Eddy Jr. The Eddys were close friends of Lovecraft's in Providence and perhaps knew his habits better than anyone other than his mother and aunts, and he would frequently visit them at their home, often after 11:00 p.m. Muriel recorded with delight the food and drink that Lovecraft enjoyed at her home: coffee, always taken with four teaspoons of sugar and swimming in cream, even on a hot day preferred over a pitcher of iced lemonade; cheese sandwiches; and a huge slice of her homemade chocolate-frosted angel cake, eaten to the last crumb with a huge smile. However, when Muriel fed her cat a can of salmon, she saw Lovecraft recoil in horror. The mere sight of seafood, fresh or cooked, made him physically ill and mentally distressed. This aversion must have been particularly difficult in a place like Providence, where clams, oysters and seafood are the native cuisine. After reading aloud his latest story "The Rats in the Walls," Lovecraft gnawed on a chicken leg Muriel offered him from her icebox. Muriel noted with approval the way this gentleman took to eating with his fingers instead of the genteel silver of his family. She records that Lovecraft reciprocated her hospitality, bringing a box of broken crackers he purchased at a deep discount at the five and dime. He explained that cheese and crackers were a staple of his daily diet. He also brought broken chunks of chocolate for the three young Eddy children, undoubtedly also bought for next to nothing. During a search for a mythical "Black Swamp" in Chepachet with Clifford Eddy, Lovecraft restored himself at a local farmhouse with gingerbread and a glass of milk. Quaint Yankee fare and sweets suited the great writer's digestion.

In 1924, Lovecraft ghost-wrote a story for Houdini called "Imprisoned with the Pharaohs," and around this time, the author moved to New York to marry Sonia Greene. The Eddys were invited to take some of Lovecraft's possessions, and when visiting the home he had shared with his aunts, Muriel noted a bathtub filled with old chocolate boxes. Lovecraft saved them, thinking they would come in handy for something someday. Mrs. Eddy left with some of them for her children to play with, as well as Lovecraft's two-burner gas plate on which he cooked his simple meals.

In 1925, Lovecraft returned to Providence, looking very thin. Lovecraft had introduced Clifford Eddy to Houdini to take over ghostwriting duties and to investigate fake spiritualists for a book called *The Cancer of Superstition* (that manuscript was recently discovered in a magic shop). When Houdini came to Providence for the last time in September 1926, it was an opportunity for the group to meet to discuss the project.

Houdini's wife, Beatrice, and niece Julia acted as his assistants onstage, and the Eddys and Lovecraft went to the show. After the show, they all dined at the Waldorf, around midnight (of course). The group ate at a long table. Beatrice Houdini had her parrot Lori on her shoulder, and Lovecraft watched as Lori drank tea from a teaspoon and nibbled on toast. Lovecraft was extremely animated that night, his mood perhaps fueled by what he consumed: half a cantaloupe with vanilla ice cream and coffee with lots of sugar. Beatrice Houdini developed food poisoning soon afterward, and Houdini would be dead from a punch to the stomach by Halloween of that year. It would be a stretch, however, to say that the food at the Waldorf was to blame. Waldorf Systems merged with Restaurant Associates around 1970, and Waldorf Lunch restaurants persisted in Providence until that time, a feat as impressive as Houdini's Chinese Water Torture Cell.

WHITE TOWER

1920s–1970s
191 Washington Street, 673 Broadway, 68 Dorrance Street, 785 Westminster Street

White Tower was a hamburger chain designed to mimic White Castle. "Take Home a Bagful" was its hopeful slogan. Its five-cent hamburgers were easy on the budget and tasty, although White Tower diversified the menu with ham sandwiches, pies and donuts. The White Tower hamburger chain was started in 1926 in Milwaukee by John E. Saxe, his son Thomas E. Saxe and Daniel J. O'Connell. Like Childs, the restaurant's white building and interior tiles were meant to suggest a hygienic atmosphere. By the late 1920s, White Tower was one of the largest chains in the country thanks to its franchise model, and there were locations in Providence next to the Majestic Theater, now the home of Trinity Repertory Company, and in Olneyville. The choice of a site was key to the success of a White Tower, and they tended to be located near trolley or bus stops. Case in point, a surviving photo of the downtown White Tower catches a trolley passing by during a blizzard in 1941.

The one-ounce burgers on a two-inch roll were served on paper napkins and came topped with mustard, chopped onions and a pickle (no ketchup). The gleaming white buildings of White Tower have many admirers, and the architect of many of the outlets, Charles Johnson, designed the restaurants with the grill in front so people could watch the hamburgers being prepared. The tiny shops typically had five stools.

The chain lost popularity after World War II, a victim of the urban decline that claimed so many Providence restaurants.

The White Tower on Washington Street during a 1941 blizzard. *Providence Public Library.*

DOWNYFLAKE DOUGHNUTS

1930s–1960s
27 Eddy Street and 173 Union Street

Franchised by Adolph Levitt, inventor of the donut machine, and his company Doughnut Corporation of America, Downyflake was one of the first chains in the United States. By 1931, there were four hundred Downyflake Restaurants nationwide.

A circa 1945 photo captured the Downyflake at the corner of Eddy and Weybosset Streets (now a 7-Eleven). The marquee shows that Downyflake was one-stop shopping for Rhode Island cuisine. It featured local Autocrat Coffee (and surely coffee milk made with Autocrat's coffee syrup) and locally canned Saltesea Clam Chowder and Oysters. Saltesea, a subsidiary of American Oyster Company of Providence, sold a popular canned chowder made with Rhode Island quahogs into the 1950s. Macaroons were also apparently a big draw at the donut shop, thanks to the sign in the spectacular rounded windows.

A wartime advertisement for the two Providence locations described them as soda fountain restaurants with counter and booth service. The advertisement depicted a mob of soldiers gathered around a donut

Downyflake Doughnuts at the corner Eddy and Weybosset Streets. *Providence Public Library.*

machine cranking out dozens at a time along with the message, "Fresh Crunchy Doughnuts Welcome Wartime Energy at Home or at the Front." Donut machines were part of the show at a Downyflake, and kids could sign up to join the National Dunking Association (splashing was taboo and any member caught getting his or her fingers wet would be subject to suspension). Members were encouraged to give the sign of the dunk upon meeting. During World War II, Downyflake donuts were distributed to soldiers overseas by the Red Cross.

There is still a Downyflake in Nantucket, last visited by me in the summer of 2018. As Dunkin' Donuts at the time of this writing considers striking the word *donuts* from its name and from the name of the Dunkin' Donuts Center in Providence (the donut chain has naming rights), it is important to remember Downyflake's history and the optimist's creed to keep our eyes on the donut and not on the hole.

THE BARNSIDER'S MILE AND A QUARTER

1983–2008
375 South Main Street

The Barnsider chain began in 1967 with a restaurant in Albany, New York, at the Colonie Shopping Center. It had a rustic barn board interior. The first Barnsider in Rhode Island opened in the Midland (later Rhode Island) Mall in 1969. That location, with wooden walls from a New York barn, closed in February 1990 after a rent increase. The Providence location opened in October 1983 in an expanded and renovated former Greek restaurant, the Mile and a Quarter House.

By the early 1980s, there were eight other Barnsiders in New York, New England and Florida. The Mile and a Quarter in the name derives from the fact that the restaurant was located a mile and a quarter from the old statehouse on Benefit Street. (Some disagree and say it was named for the length of a horse race.) Benefit Street itself is called the mile of history.

Once upon a time, exposed brick, hanging plants and shiny brass were the makings of a fresh and exciting new place to dine. On a Saturday night, there was often a wait of an hour or more for a table, and the upstairs lounge was hopping. The original menu was printed on a wooden cutting board and had only a few items, like onion soup, the salad bar and the top sirloin. Its

mile and a quarter house

*an elegant adventure in
Continental dining
with a Greek flavor!*

open daily 11 am to 1 am, weekend to 2 am
closed on Sundays for the Summer

334 So. Water St. Prov.   273-8100

Left: The first Mile and a Quarter House was a Greek restaurant. *Author's collection.*

Below: Dinner choices included the Barnsider's top sirloin, "the steak that made us famous! No fat, no bone, just great taste." *Fred Goodwin.*

Menu from the Barnsider's Mile and a Quarter. *Fred Goodwin.*

The Barnsider's Mile and a Quarter after it closed in 2008. *Christopher Scott Martin/Quahog.org*

reputation for great steaks was further burnished by a steak sandwich called the Iowa Hawkeye: sliced sirloin, served open-faced with garlic butter on a baguette with a side of corn bread. In its early years, the Barnsider served a lot of Mexican and Southwest-themed dishes to complement its prime steaks. It was probably best known for its excellent salad bar, which constituted a meal in itself. A former manager remembers that the wealthy "East Side ladies" would smuggle in doggy bags and help themselves to hunks of Cheddar cheese and other salad bar fixings to take home for another meal. The Barnsider had a clever old-fashioned bicycle logo, used in its signage and menus. Today, the Barnsider's Mile and a Quarter House is still best remembered for that salad bar. So what was in a salad bar that still causes so many people to wax rhapsodic and to tempt otherwise honest East Siders to surreptitious doggy bag behavior? Here is what you could pile on your (chilled) plate, as far as I have been able to piece together: mixed greens, broccoli heads, cauliflower heads, carrots, red onion rings, celery sticks, cherry tomatoes, sliced cucumbers, bacon bits, grated Parmesan, shredded red cabbage, cheese (big blocks), bread that you sliced yourself and blue cheese dressing with actual chunks of blue cheese.

Rhode Island's longest-running mystery theater, Murder on Us, started its performances with dinner at the Barnsider's Mile and a Quarter in 1992 and continued to perform there until the restaurant's closing. Today, the theater continues to perform at Bravo at 123 Empire Street, owned by former Barnsider manager Fred Goodwin. Bravo celebrates the traditions of the Barnsider and other lost Providence restaurants and even serves a Bravo Hawkeye. The Barnsider Mile and a Quarter closed in June 2008, reportedly because acceptable terms could not be reached on a new lease in a bad year for the American economy.

The Barnsider in Albany is still going strong.

AMSTERDAM'S BAR & ROTISSERIE

1990–1996
76 South Main Street

Amsterdam's was a mini-chain with two locations in New York City and two in Rhode Island. The Newport restaurant opened in the summer of 1988 at 509 Thames Street in the location of the former Southern Cross, and

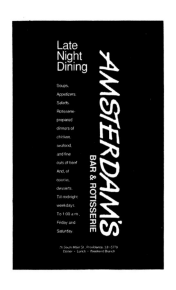

An ad for Amsterdam's focused on late-night dining. *Author's collection.*

the Providence restaurant followed in April 1990, importing a new level of cool to the city. A few chic friends of mine worked there and made great tips. Amsterdam's featured chickens roasting on a spit, and the reasonably priced chicken dinners complemented with green herb or sesame ginger tahini sauces came with superb french fries and a salad. Reviewers at the time were struck by the all-black outfits worn by the servers, including, shockingly, Spandex. Providence had come a long way from the nurse-like outfits worn by the servers at Childs.

The Providence Amsterdam's achieved local immortality when issues arose with city hall after Mayor Buddy Cianci was denied entry at the rope one night by a doorman. That incident recently achieved international infamy when it was discussed in episode 14 ("Renaissance Man") of the popular podcast *Crimetown*. Amsterdam's stayed open until 2:00 a.m. and featured live music in the late evening. In his autobiography, Cianci explains that on December 16, 1991, he went to Amsterdam's with his girlfriend, sister and brother-in-law and was told there was a cover charge of five dollars per person for those wanting to listen to the music. Cianci argued that he was there to dine and not for the music. He conceded that he didn't like paying a cover charge but claimed what happened next was unrelated. He says he observed that the place was so full people could barely move. Accordingly, he called the fire department, which responded to the scene and temporarily closed Amsterdam's for overcrowding. It had a capacity of 114 people, and there were many more than that inside.

Later, in his autobiography, Cianci also added more fuel to the fire with an unsubstantiated allegation that Amsterdam's had been serving alcohol to minors, including his daughter. The restaurant paid a $250 fee for the overcrowding and did not ultimately lose its liquor license as had been feared. Cianci admitted that he went there many times for dinner afterward and it was "considerably less crowded." Amsterdam's closed in 1996, and Parkside Rotisserie opened in the space shortly afterward. Parkside is a must-visit stop for anyone doing a *Crimetown* tour of Providence.

6
Renaissance

JOE'S UPSTAIRS

1975–1977
66 Mathewson Street

Joe's Upstairs was located at 66 Mathewson Street, in a building that is no longer standing. Short-lived but still discussed, Dewey Dufresne's Joe's Upstairs is credited as the first locavore restaurant in Providence, with an emphasis on the best local ingredients. I would argue that Miss Dutton's Green Room (with its use of produce from Flora Dutton's farm) and Johnson's Hummocks (with its lobster tanks in Wickford) were earlier locavore restaurants, but certainly Joe's sparked a renaissance in a by then moribund restaurant city. Joe's was an incubator for the underground scene in Providence that created repercussions in the city for decades to come.

In a somewhat industrial atmosphere of steel chairs, chrome lamps and Formica booths, softened by an exposed brick wall, Joe's served appetizers including cheese and crackers, a bagel with chive cream cheese and fried smelts, which, concededly, do not sound very groundbreaking. However, the freshness of the lettuce in the salad, showcased in a clear glass bowl, caused raptures in restaurant reviewer Michael Janusonis, who commented it was the "freshest, crispest lettuce this wide of a garden patch."

Curiously, Dewey Dufresne's name never appeared in the review, and people must have wondered who Joe was. When I spoke to Dewey about his Providence restaurants, he enthused to me about the great self-descriptive names of old Rhode Island diners like the Ever Ready. Indeed, his grandfather ran a donut shop in Central Falls called Ever Good. Perhaps Dewey was going for that approach in giving his places names like Joe's Upstairs, Joe's Downstairs and Joe's Old Abandoned Grocery Store. His most famous naming exercise, however, may be his son, chef Wylie Dufresne.

Joe's was not afraid of bold sauces with a kick for the Shrimp George (spicy tomato) or the West Indian Barbecue Chicken (a hot chutney of pineapple, tomato and onion). Little twists of brilliance abounded, like a sprinkle of Parmesan cheese on the broccoli or the coffee liqueur in the whipped cream on the Greek honey walnut cake. Forward looking, Joe's also evinced a knowing nostalgia with dishes like sautéed chicken livers, onion and bacon and beverages like Dr. Brown's Cel-Ray Soda and raspberry lime rickeys. Joe's had a thing for bananas, whether in a frozen banana daiquiri or, for dessert, a baked Jamaican banana in a butter, honey and rum sauce with cashews. Dufresne would buy the ingredients daily, spurring the chefs to spontaneity.

George Germon was the cook and helped design the restaurant, and Johanne Killeen was the pastry chef, famed at Joe's for her amazing brownies. Perhaps in response to the experience at Joe's Upstairs, which was a creative but not a financial success, George and Johanne later opened their restaurant Al Forno in a tiny space on Steeple Street, the few tables fanning an insatiable demand for their grilled pizza and baked pasta in the pink that still has not subsided today, even after a move to its own two-story building near the hurricane barrier. Thinking small worked so well for them that they later opened a lost restaurant actually called Tini in the former New Yorker diner, where Birch is located today.

Dewey took out a billboard visible to drivers heading into the city down Thomas Street from the East Side to draw attention to the restaurant, and there was a busy lunch crowd, but only the adventurous dined in the city. Happenings like a screening of the film *Dead City* by Marc Kehoe were not enough to save Joe's Upstairs. Talk to certain old-timers about the dismal state of downtown in the 1970s, though, and they will smile knowingly and say that it was their favorite time in Providence because of Joe's Upstairs.

JOE'S OLD ABANDONED GROCERY STORE

1969–1970s
163 Benefit Street

Parallel to Dewey Dufresne's existence as a downtown restaurateur was his legendary reputation as "Mr. Sandwich." Joe's Downstairs was his pop-up sandwich place downtown, but Dewey's more enduring sandwich fame comes from Joe's Old Abandoned Grocery Store on Benefit Street, located quite literally in an old bodega-style grocery store.

The uniqueness of Dewey's sandwiches is apparent even in the signature "Joe." It was kosher pastrami and melted swiss with a special mustard called Nance's that was sweet and hot and came in small bottles. Dewey's sandwich shop was the biggest purchaser of Nance's mustard. Dewey was hot on warm fillings for the sandwiches, heated in steam machines. He was also a great believer in celery salt as a condiment, not surprising given his soft spot for Rhode Island diners and their Saugy franks dusted with celery salt. There was a big butcher block table in the middle of the space with a barrel of sour pickles. A Dufresne establishment needed music, and there was a vacant lot next door where Scott Hamilton played.

After Dewey sold the sandwich shop around the time Joe's Upstairs closed, it became Geoff's Superlative Sandwiches, and that barrel of sour pickles remained in roughly the same spot until this year when Geoff's finally moved out of the old abandoned grocery store to a new address. Dewey Dufresne is still making innovative sandwiches and news in New York City.

LEO'S

1974–1994
99 Chestnut Street

John Rector came to Providence to attend Brown University as a member of the class of 1971. He soon started working at the Graduate Center Bar at the Rhode Island School of Design, where he became acquainted with many of the major figures of the rising Providence art, music and food scene.

In September 1974, Rector opened Leo's on Chestnut Street in the jewelry district. Rector's embrace of local artists showed in the décor. A

A fittingly sudsy ad for Leo's. *Author's collection.*

distinctive feature of Leo's was the nineteen-foot painting by Dan Gosch, a mural of people in a bar, including elderly twin sisters eating hot dogs. People often thought, incorrectly, that the mural depicted customers, but Gosch used advertisements from magazines for the faces. Later, a gallery of oil on Masonite portraits by Gosch, 135 in all, was added to the back of the bar. The bar itself was a mahogany masterpiece over 125 years old that came from McGovern's, the oldest pub in Rhode Island. Dewey Dufresne had purchased it at auction. Rector was known as Mr. Suds in Providence because he sold beer, while Dufresne was known as Mr. Sandwich. It's a sign of their groundbreaking status as revitalizers in town that they were recognized by these nicknames.

Leo's was known as a conversation bar, and although it had a television, it was seldom turned on. The later revitalization of the city owed much to the first colonizers of abandoned spaces downtown who came to Leo's to discuss the issues of the day and to dream of a better future, often sketched on a Leo's napkin. Leo's was immediately successful because there was a need for a young bar in Providence. Leo's size did not allow for much in the way of entertainment, although in the summer it hosted asphalt picnics with music outside that were very popular.

Painter Bunny Harvey and a friend were allowed by Rector to paint the wall opposite the bar with blackboard paint, and she and her friend had an ongoing collaborative and evolving chalk mural that engaged them and customers for several years.

When Leo's closed in 1994, it had been open nearly twenty years and had evolved from a bar that served the best chili in town (Bunny Harvey confirms the chili and burgers were "totally reliable") to a place with a full lunch and dinner menu. A given night might find Governor Ed DiPrete or John F. Kennedy Jr. in the crowd, although probably not together.

Its humorous slogans like "underlooking Route 95" and "life without Leo's would suck" were appropriate to Leo's counterculture origins. The ribs were favorites, but the Leo's recipe included in the *Rhode Island Cooks* recipe collection was Phillipe and Jorge's Chicken. Phillipe and Jorge are Chip Young and Rudy Cheeks, respectively, of *The Phoenix's New Paper*. They collaborated with Linda Bigelow of Leo's on the recipe, and it was a colorful Mediterranean boneless chicken breast dish, with fennel, red bell pepper and green and black olives in a sauce of white wine, Pernod and tomato paste. The garlic soup was another popular dish.

Rector later the opened the Groceria on Weybosset Street, a combination grocery store and restaurant that hoped to fill a need for a downtown grocery store to cater to the people following the Leo's pioneers in moving to the new apartments and condominiums in former commercial buildings. Unfortunately, there were not yet enough downtown residents to justify a grocery store and the Groceria, a noble concept, did not last.

JULIENNE'S

1974–1980
124 Washington Street

Julienne's was only open for a few years, from 1974 to 1980, but it has a surprisingly enduring reputation. "Pure Americana," commented one person I spoke to. Someone else remembered the brightly colored refrigerators, of all things. At a time when Providence had become overrun with fast-food restaurants and the gracious Shepard Tea Room and Miss Dutton's were lost, young RISD Architecture graduate Julie Peterson opened her self-service (but with cloth napkins) lunch place. In a second-floor space, formerly occupied by Chen's Chinese restaurant, she exposed the brick walls and original floorboards. The cheery interior design included yellow chairs, green-checked upholstery on the booths and windows open to the views of the Dreyfus Hotel across the street. The choices for hot and cold soups of the day were presented on an easel at the top of the stairs.

For three dollars, diners could have homemade tomato soup with fresh tomatoes, herbs and sour cream and a salad with a dressing full of marinated vegetables like mushrooms, tomatoes and green pepper. There was a second salad dressing based on a recipe from Julie's mother, who had worked as a Crockerette with the Betty Crocker Test Kitchen. Little baskets held a choice of sliced pumpernickel or Italian bread with a bowl of butter. The food was prepared in an open kitchen behind the butcher block counter from which the soups and salads were served. A server wheeled the dessert cart to the table with temptations like a bowl of fruit compote, a cheese selection or homemade cake and cookies.

In March 1979, Julie offered a cooking class for men at Julienne's. On Friday, August 1, 1980, Julie Peterson announced she was closing her restaurant and traveling to Europe to observe the grape harvest in Italy and perhaps later to spend the winter working at a Paris restaurant. She also speculated that she might return to Providence to open a smaller restaurant and dreamed of writing a cookbook and hosting a television cooking show. The hoped for Julienne's sequel in Providence alas never occurred because Julie remained in Italy. However, she later wrote a delightful children's book, *Caterina, the Clever Farm Girl: A Tale from Italy*, with drawings by her husband, Enzo Giannini.

BLUEPOINT

1978–1996
99 North Main Street

Bluepoint opened at the bottom of College Hill, near the intersection of Thomas and North Main Streets, in 1978. Bluepoint had an unassuming storefront façade, but there was a mural of fish swimming on an exterior side wall that hinted at the glories within. Not since the heyday of the shore dinner hall at Fields Point or Johnson's Hummocks had there been a restaurant in the city so dedicated to obtaining and serving the freshest local seafood. In 1980, owner Paul Inveen was joined at Bluepoint by chef Maureen Pothier, a Rhode Island native and recent graduate of the Rhode Island School of Design's culinary program. The pair later married. Pothier started as a prep cook at Bluepoint but made the transformation to chef after a revelatory period of studying with Madeleine Kamman in 1982.

BLUEPOINT

⚓

The Finest Seafood
Restaurant in Providence

99 No. Main St. Prov.   272-6145

Bluepoint was the finest seafood
restaurant in Providence since
Johnson's Hummocks. *Author's collection.*

Pothier was one of the first Rhode Island chefs to use bycatch, underutilized fish species that abound in Rhode Island waters, and Bluepoint's seafood came straight from the docks. Fish was often simply grilled over herb-strewn charcoal, and Pothier broadened diners' palates by introducing them to skate, shad roe and raw sea urchin.

Brown University's student guidebook *Divine Providence* called Bluepoint "a high-class, loose-hipped bar for the businessman elite, and the rest of us too." Perhaps only the expense account crowd could afford the seafood platter, but the homemade sausage was in anyone's budget. Jacqueline Kennedy Onassis ate at Bluepoint with her son, John, when he was a student at Brown. Ringo Starr, Michael Jackson, Bernadette Peters, Jimmy Carter, Jane Fonda and I also dined there.

Pothier contributed a recipe for Bluepoint's Red Quahog Chowder to *Rhode Island Cooks*, a collection published in 1992 by the American Cancer Society Rhode Island Division. The ingredients included ten pounds of fresh quahogs in the shell, basil, oregano, Italian parsley and grated orange rind, dry red wine and vermouth. She wisely recommended making the soup base in advance and adding chopped quahogs at serving time and cooking until just heated though to keep the clams tender. Her method for opening quahogs was to steam them in a roasting pan in a 350-degree oven until just opening.

Bluepoint closed in 1996 because the owners of the building wanted to demolish it for another project. Pothier moved into restaurant consulting and teaching and is now department chair of the Culinary Arts Program at Johnson & Wales University.

IN PROV

1987–1994
Fleet Center, 50 Kennedy Plaza

John Elkhay's In Prov had tables in the galleria of the Fleet Center and an open kitchen. In the era of Oliver Stone's *Wall Street*, it was appropriate that an ambitious new restaurant would open in a bank building. Such a mixture of commerce and dining had not been seen in Providence since the Shepard Tea Room. Reflecting the reality of Providence's dining scene at the time, the restaurant offered a full lunch menu but in the evening served only tapas and desserts. Elkhay was the first chef to introduce tapas to Providence. However, he used the term in the sense of appetizer-sized portions rather than Spanish food.

In Prov helped launch what has become one of Rhode Island's great restaurant success stories. John Elkhay graduated from Johnson & Wales in 1977. He worked at restaurants in New York and Nantucket and was executive chef at Guy Abelson's Café in the Barn restaurant on Route 6 in Seekonk from 1980 to 1983. Housed in a barn on three acres of property, Café in the Barn was destroyed by a fire in February 1991.

Elkhay teamed with Abelson to open In Prov in 1987. Its menu was a little Southwest (Santa Fe shrimp with blue crab cakes) and a little Asian. Probably In Prov's most talked about dish was the Lo Mein Yu Hung Lo. It consisted of wok-fired broccoli, red pepper, snow peas and mushrooms with grilled chicken and swordfish, in a sauce composed of raspberry vinegar, ginger, sesame oil, molasses and soy sauce, served over lo mein noodles and decorated with black sesame seeds.

In 1988, when scones had become all the rage in Providence, In Prov's triangular scones with sherry-soaked raisins and accompanied by raspberry jam proved so popular that the restaurant would sell out by 9:00 a.m. The six dozen baked each day were neatly stackable and reserved in paper bags for customers in the know, a little Gordon Gecko excess in the Wall Street of Providence.

IN·PROV

TAPAS · ROTISSERIE & BAR

"Top Ten Places in the Country for Dinners to Go"
Bon Apetit 1991

"Rhode Island's Best Caterer"
Rhode Island Monthly 1991

"Best Designed Restaurant"
Restaurant & Institutions 1987

WHAT ELSE DO YOU WANT?
Open Late on Show Nights!!

Fleet Center • 50 Kennedy Plaza • Providence • 351•8770

In Prov introduced tapas to Providence. *Author's collection.*

In 1990, a summer slowdown hurt business, but In Prov pulled through and survived for several more years. In the years since, through his Chow Fun Group, Elkhay oversees an empire that includes the Harry's Bar & Burger chain, a catering arm that served President Obama in Newport and XO Café on North Main Street, which became another lost restaurant of Providence in June 2018.

DOWNCITY DINER

1990–2011
111 Eddy Street

Anthony Salemme had already built a following before he opened Downcity Diner in 1990. He subleased the kitchen at Custom House Tavern and provided the food at that now lost tavern. It had always been his dream to run a restaurant of his own. Anthony, who studied at Johnson & Wales, was only twenty-seven when he opened Downcity Diner. Fran Whiting's Plaza Grille on Federal Hill is one of Anthony's favorite lost restaurants and perhaps was an inspiration for the kind of restaurant he wanted to open.

Originally, the entrance to Downcity Diner was on Eddy Street and there were only forty-eight seats. Anthony expanded into the front space in 1992 and added a bar. (Before then, Downcity was BYOB.) The restaurant served breakfast until 2000. Downcity Diner was a pioneer in that area in that time, and city hall was not yet committed to helping new restaurants in the city. Eddie & Son, the Woolworth Lunch Counter and Pot au Feu were the few restaurants open at that time.

The restaurant's name would have an impact on how Providence referred to itself for decades to come, so it is edifying to discover how it was selected. The restaurant was going to be called the Downtown Diner until someone suggested that Downcity is how old-timers would have described going to that area near the Outlet to shop. (The Outlet had burned to the ground a few years before.) The name Downcity Diner was then adopted for its nostalgic resonance. Notably, this was before the "Downcity" plan and branding effort were adopted by Providence. I have been told that the commission, chaired by architect Andres Duany, may have come up with that name for the plan because it held its meetings at Downcity Diner. Downcity was a wonderful name for a diner, but the term has had less success in the attempt to revive it as shorthand catchall for the shopping and restaurant district of the city.

The Downcity Diner's menu art depicted a stylized Providence skyline. *Anthony Salemme.*

BREAKFAST

A.M. SPECIAL		**CEREAL & FRUIT**	1.50
2 eggs, homefries, toast & coffee/tea	1.99		
with bacon or honeyham	2.99	**COFFEE CAKE**	1.00
SUNNYSIDE SANDWICH		**BAGEL & CREAM CHEESE**	.95
1 egg, honeyham, cheddar on bolo	1.75	**MUFFIN**	.75
3 EGG OMELETTE		**PORTUGUESE CORNBREAD TOAST**	
with cheddar or gruyere cheese	2.95	a dense sourdough	.75
with ham, peppers & onions	3.25		
with spinach, roasted peppers		**CINNAMON TOAST**	.75
& cheddar	3.75		
served with homefries and toast		**SIDE OF HONEY HAM or BACON**	1.50
WEYBOSSET HASH		**SIDE OF HOME FRIES**	.75
corned beef hash, 2 eggs, toast	3.95		
SWEET BREAD FRENCH TOAST			
with butter & syrup	2.75		
BUTTERMILK PANCAKES			
4 cakes with butter & syrup	2.75		
4 cakes with fruit compote	3.50		

TO • GO
331.9217

DRINKS

COFFEE		**COFFEE MILK OR CHOCOLATE MILK**	.85
chocolate almond or traditional	.85	**YACHT CLUB SODA**	.85
JUICE		black cherry, grape, cream, ginger ale,	
cranberry, orange, apple, grapefruit	.95	original seltzer, lemon seltzer, raspberry seltzer	
MILK	.75	**COLA, DIET COLA, LEMON-LIME**	.85

To-go & catering service. Downcity Diner is available for private functions.
Downcity Diner 111 Eddy Street, Providence, RI 02903 (401) 331-9217

LUNCH

SOUP OF THE DAY	1.95	**MOM'S MEATLOAF SANDWICH**	
		with mayo & lettuce on Portuguese	
TEXAS BEEF CHILI		cornbread	3.95
with cheese & onion	2.50		
		HONEY HAM & CHEDDAR SANDWICH	
SEASONAL GARDEN SALAD		with mustard on rye	3.95
romano, celery seed or french dressing	2.50		
		NEW MEXICAN TUNA SANDWICH	
CURRIED CHICKEN SALAD		with black olive salsa on cornbread	3.95
with apples & walnuts	4.50		
		BURGERS	
METRO CHICKEN SALAD		naked	3.50
caesar salad with roasted chicken	4.95	with cheddar or gruyere cheese	4.00
		with bacon & cheese	4.75
WARM ORIENTAL BEEF SALAD		on Portuguese bolo roll	
marinated beef, carrots, mushrooms,		All sandwiches served with cole slaw	
broccoli in a light teriyaki sauce	4.50	& homefries	
CITY CLUB SANDWICH		**SHEPHERDS PIE**	
smoked turkey, bacon, lettuce, tomato		old fashioned meat pie with potato &	
& mayo on toasted wheat	4.75	vegetable, served with side salad	4.95
SMOKED TURKEY SANDWICH		**MOM'S MEATLOAF**	
with cranberry orange relish	3.95	with mashed potatoes, gravy	
with melted cheese, mayo & mustard	4.25	& vegetable	4.95
both on Portuguese cornbread			
ROAST BEEF SANDWICH		**NEW ENGLAND CHEESE PIE**	
with creamy horseradish sauce on rye	4.25	made with Vermont cheddar, walnuts &	
		onions, served with side salad	4.50

ASK ABOUT OUR DAILY BLUEPLATES

DESSERT

PIE	1.95	**JELLO**	1.25
PIE A LA MODE	2.50	**ICE CREAM**	1.50
CAKE	2.25	**COOKIES**	.75

Printed on recycled paper.

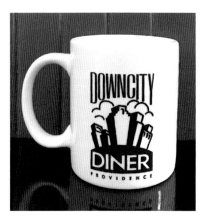

Above: The original Downcity Diner menu. *Left*: A coffee mug from Downcity Diner. *Anthony Salemme.*

The customers were always a diverse bunch. Older people from Grace Church, lawyers and judges, local celebrities and couples in town for a show were in the mix, and Downcity was also a very welcoming home to Providence's gay and lesbian community.

My particular menu favorite was the meatloaf sandwich served on a dense sourdough-like Portuguese corn bread (made with white corn flour). When Anthony sent me the meatloaf recipe for inclusion in this book, I chuckled at its simplicity, particularly the gravy (out of a jar). Originally, Anthony did everything, including acting as chef. In 1996, he took on partner Paul Childs. They sold the restaurant in 2004, and there was a fire in 2006 (reportedly caused by a beef brisket) that was so severe the building had to be demolished. Downcity's new owners reopened in 2007 at 50 Weybosset Street across from the Arcade. That reinvention of the restaurant was featured on an episode of Gordon Ramsay's *Kitchen Nightmares* in 2011 but closed later that year, despite the celebrity intervention.

For many, Downcity Diner will always be remembered as the restaurant that truly made them believe in the renaissance of downtown Providence as a dining destination.

7

Neighborhood

FARMSTEAD

2003–2014
186 Wayland Avenue

Matt Jennings may be the first chef in Providence to be recognizable solely by his finger tattoos. Raised in Jamaica Plain, Massachusetts, he enrolled in New England Culinary Institute in Montpelier, Vermont, after kitchen stints in Nantucket and Phoenix. He worked at Formaggio Kitchen, a food shop in Cambridge, where he met his wife, Kate. His mother retired to Little Compton, and while visiting her, he and Kate toured Providence and decided to open a store there. In 2003, they bought the former Cheese Shop in Wayland Square, about a mile from downtown, and proceeded to educate Providence about cheese. The couple began by hosting cheese, charcuterie and wine parties. Eventually, they expanded into the space next door for a wine bar but found they also had room for a restaurant, La Laiterie, which opened in 2006. Matt decided to try his hand at being the chef; Kate was the baker, and initially, the menu consisted of cheese plates, house-made charcuterie and pâtés and pasta dishes like macaroni with heirloom tomato sauce and fresh chevre. Kate had to prepare the desserts in advance to be out of the small kitchen before the dinner service.

A satellite location at 225A Westminster Street, Downcity Farmstead, was open from 2008 to 2011 and had some of the best sandwiches in the city, like the cheesemonger's grilled cheese. There also was scrapple made with local pork and cornmeal from Kenyon's. Farmstead's signature dish may have been its mac and cheese penne in a blend of Gruyère, sharp Cheddar and Brie, brightened by fresh thyme and nutmeg.

When *Bizarre Foods* came to town in 2012 to profile Farmstead, the health inspector had temporarily halted the sale of cured meats and cheese. Somehow Matt kept his cool, which was perhaps why he was so frequently nominated for the James Beard Foundation's award for Best Chef Northeast. Ben Sukle, later of Oberlin and Birch, was chef de cuisine at Farmstead and La Laiterie from around 2006 to 2011.

Matt and Kate closed Farmstead in 2014 to open their dream restaurant Townsman in Boston's Greenway, making Farmstead one of the rare lost Providence restaurants to close because its chef left to conquer a bigger city. Matt's cookbook *Homegrown: Cooking from My New England Roots* is a paean to the foods of his childhood and has two clam chowder recipes, one made with clams and squid (and squid ink crackers), the other his mother's version with "no squid or other crap." Fortunately, I was able to taste the squid version and Matt's brown bread at Townsman before it too became a lost restaurant in July 2018. The Salted Slate carries on the former Farmstead space.

MEDITERRANEO

2007–2015
134 Atwells Avenue

Anyone driving from downtown under the pinecone arch to Atwells Avenue on Federal Hill on a summer evening would be captivated by the cosmopolitan sight of French doors open to the sidewalk at Mediterraneo and the view of diners feasting under the yellow-and-blue-striped awning. It was a scene evoking Venice or Florence or the stretch of Sixth Avenue in New York's Greenwich Village where Del Posto and Da Silvano sit side by side. A prime location for outdoor seating, a see and be seen clientele and excellent Italian food made the restaurant an instant success.

In a building that previously had served as another Italian restaurant, the Arch, Mediterraneo was opened in 2007 by the Marrocco Group. Gianfranco Marrocco first came to Providence from Italy on a vacation with his father. When his father chose to remain, the future Federal Hill

Doors open on a sunny day at Mediterraneo on Federal Hill. *Christopher Scott Martin/Quahog.org.*

restaurateur enrolled in school and began working at Federal Hill's Angelo's Civita Farnese. Marrocco returned to Italy in his early twenties, returning to Providence in 1986. In 1992, he opened Caffe Dolce Vita, bringing a taste of the Italian sweet life to DePasquale Plaza. In partnership with other investors, he graced Federal Hill with Mediterraneo. Marrocco also was responsible for Gepetto's Pizzeria and the boutique Hotel Dolce Villa, and he was proud of employing many Italian immigrants at his establishments.

Standouts on the menu at Mediterraneo were the Spaghetti à la Vongole (showing off local littlenecks), chicken piccata, lobster ravioli from Venda covered in a delectable pink sauce and mozzarella in carrozza, breaded pan-fried cheese served in tomato sauce. The place had a modern feel with old country flourishes like house-made limoncello. Mediterraneo was a place where you might see Mayor Buddy Cianci holding court or Danny DeVito trying to get in after hours. Mediterraneo closed in 2015, when the building was sold. Massimo later opened in its space.

ALFREDO'S

1962–1993
280 Thayer Street

Around 1962, Alfredo and Mary Andreozzi sold their interest in the Welcome Spa owned by the Andreozzi brothers on Chalkstone Avenue and opened Alfredo's on Thayer Street. Over the years, IHOP, McDonald's and other fast-food restaurants had begun to take over the Brown University college district, and Alfredo's was a mom-and-pop survivor. In 1984, Alfredo's expanded into a neighboring space, adding a bar. At the time, the menu included brook trout meuniere, baked haddock marinara, baked stuffed shrimp and six veal dishes, including one with layers of mozzarella and prosciutto in a marsala wine sauce.

It was the kind of place where one could order raw bar littlenecks or Rhode Island snail salad made with oil and vinegar, red pepper flakes, oregano, celery and onions. A late-night menu surely appealed to the student crowd craving sandwiches, antipasto or mud pie (coffee ice cream and whipped cream covered in fudge and nuts in an Oreo crust).

On one wall of Alfredo's, Bert Crenca, a member of the Andreozzi family and later the founder and artistic director of AS220, painted a mural in honor of his family's history. It depicts the hometown of Diomede and Anita Andreozzi, the founders of the Welcome Spa, including the church where the couple was married. A former student of Bert's rescued it from the back of a truck when Alfredo's was demolished, and he has been told it now hangs in her house. After Alfredo Andreozzi Sr. died, his wife and children continued to run Alfredo's. By the 1980s, grandchildren were working there too.

Bert Crenca's brother Daniel worked as a cook at Alfredo's and has recently been serving the old Alfredo's lasagna recipe at his own restaurant Nico Bella's (briefly in the old Eddie & Son space). From what I tasted, that lasagna was well worth a revival. Daniel also served the treasured ham recipe from the Welcome Spa, and as I savored it one afternoon, he explained that Italian American spas like the Welcome were the daytime equivalent of bars. It was where men went to read the paper, have a coffee and eat a ham sandwich on a Crugnale hard roll. It's wonderful when a taste of ham comes with a history lesson, and it's also wonderful that times change.

RUE DE L'ESPOIR

1976–2015
99 Hope Street

Founded by Deborah Norman in 1976, Rue de L'Espoir (French for Hope Street), better known as simply "The Rue," was originally conceived as an American bistro that would serve quiche and crêpes.

The original menu was small and modestly typed in lower case. It offered everything you could want from a little French bistro with forty-five seats: chicken liver pâté, quiche lorraine, onion soup, a spinach, mushroom and bacon salad with blue cheese and savory crêpes filled with Gruyère, sour cream, ratatouille or onions and mushroom. Deborah was the cook for the first three years.

A graduate of Hope High School and the University of Rhode Island, Norman began her restaurant career at a lost lounge on North Main Street called the Incredible Organ. Over the years, the Rue lost some of its French focus, but a great salad, French onion soup or pâté could always be ordered, preceded by hot bread and sweet butter on the table.

Rue de l'Espoir meant fine French cooking to many. *Christopher Scott Martin/Quahog.org.*

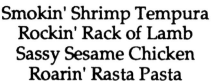

Above: An ad for the Rue stressed that it served more than just quiche. *Author's collection.*

Right: Even the bathrooms were romantic at the Rue. *Christopher Scott Martin/Quahog.org*

An advertisement from 1989 boasted about Smokin' Shrimp Tempura, Rockin' Rack of Lamb, Sassy Sesame Chicken and Roarin' Rasta Pasta to demonstrate that the Rue's interpretation of creative cooking and stylish dining had evolved with the times. Norman eventually expanded the restaurant to seat seventy-five, with room for an additional forty in the bar. It served breakfast, lunch and dinner, seven days a week. The lemon ricotta griddlecakes were a breakfast standout.

When it closed on August 9, 2015, the Rue had been serving for thirty-nine years. Testimonials written by customers in a memory book revealed that the Rue had been life-enhancing in a way that only a few restaurants manage.

Chef Champe Spiedel, a James Beard nominee for best regional chef, and his wife, Lisa, moved their restaurant Persimmon from Bristol to the storied terroir of the Rue in 2016.

Recipes

Miss Dutton's Baked Swordfish with Herb Butter

3–4 pounds swordfish (cut in one piece 3 inches thick)
½ teaspoon mustard
Salt
Pepper
Bacon fat or butter

Rub mustard on top and bottom of fish. Salt and pepper to taste. Brown in bacon fat or butter and then bake in frying pan or casserole in 400-degree oven about 12 minutes per pound, basting frequently with butter or drippings. Slice down and serve with herb butter.

Herb Butter

½ cup butter or Oleo
¼ cup finely chopped parsley
1 tablespoon chopped dill or chives
2 tablespoons lemon juice

Melt butter with herbs and lemon juice in a saucepan and drizzle over swordfish before serving.

Swordfish cooked in this way is very moist and juicy

Miss Dutton's Baked Chocolate Pudding

3 cups milk
1 ¼ cups stale bread or cake, cubed or crumbed
¼ cup sugar
½ teaspoon salt
2 squares chocolate, melted
1 teaspoon vanilla extract
2 eggs, beaten

Scald milk and pour over bread crumbs. Combine sugar, salt and melted chocolate and vanilla. Add eggs to first two mixtures. Pour into buttered casserole and bake 1 ¼ hours at 350 degrees or until firm. Serve with hard sauce.

Miss Dutton's Hard Sauce

½ cup butter or Oleo
2 cups confectioner's sugar, sifted
2 teaspoons vanilla extract
2 tablespoons rum flavoring
2 tablespoons hot milk

Cream butter, add sugar and flavoring gradually. When well blended, add hot milk slowly and beat until fluffy.

Childs Butter Cakes
From Walter Crocker, window griddle chef

4 ounces yeast
1 quart warm water
1 pound sugar
1 pound shortening
2 ounces salt
3 quarts water
12 pounds bread flour

Mix all this as you would for bread, allow to rise and shape into 10 dozen cakes roughly the size of English muffins. Refrigerate, and then, as wanted, cook them on a griddle in the window while wearing a tall chef's hat, five minutes on one side, and three minutes on the other. For toasted butter cakes, split and griddle cakes until the insides are crispy brown. Slather with butter and wash down with coffee.

Shepard Tea Room Date Nut Bread
From Donald Bianco

This bread, made fresh in the third-floor bakery, was baked in special larger loaf pans with straight sides. The 4x3½x16-inch loaves were sliced ³/₈-inch thick. Three slices were sandwiched with two generous portions of cream cheese, which was softened with a little milk and lemon juice. The triple sandwich was then cut diagonally into four wedges. The luncheon plate was lined with iceberg lettuce leaves, and the date nut quarters were placed with each triangle facing peak up forming an X on the lettuce leaves. Large cubes of Jello were placed between the bread quarters, and the plate was garnished with carrot curls or fresh fruit.

20 ounces pitted dates, cut in quarters
1¼ cups boiling water
3 tablespoons butter, softened
6 ounces granulated sugar
2 teaspoons salt

4 teaspoons baking soda
1 cup chopped walnuts
2 large eggs, beaten
2 tablespoons honey
14 ounces bread flour

Soak dates in boiling water for 10 minutes. Put into mixing bowl, add butter and mix with the paddle on medium speed for another 10 minutes or until jam-like consistency.

Add all remaining ingredients except flour. Mix for an additional 3 minutes, scraping bowl as needed. Add flour and blend well.

Divide into three lightly greased and floured foil loaf tins.

Bake at 300 degrees for 75 minutes. Invert onto parchment paper, leaving pan on until cooled.

Shepard Tea Room Brownies (Candy Type)
From Donald Bianco

Author's note: This recipe is from an original Shepard Tea Room recipe card and is reprinted exactly for an authentic window into the past and tearoom methods. It has not been tested for home use but is wonderful to read nonetheless.

Shortening-MFB-Primex 1½ lb.
Chocolate (dark) 13 oz.

Melt together over double boiler. Have mix very hot.

Sugar 2 lb. 10 oz.
Whole eggs—fresh 12

Mix sugar and eggs on second speed for 1–2 minutes.

Cake flour—sifted 13 oz.

Add flour to sugar and egg mixture all at once.

Chopped walnuts 1 lb.

Add to above, then add hot chocolate mixture.

Pour into two greased 18 x 12 pans. Handle mix very fast as it will set up. Bake at 350 degrees for 20 to 25 min. Do not over-bake as product will dry out. Bake only until product is firm.
For Restaurant use—leave brownies un-iced. Cut 35 pieces per sheet.
For Retail use—ice with Chocolate Fondant (Recipe #48) Use 1 lb. per sheet. Cut 35 pieces per sheet.

Downyflake Peach Donut Shortcake

Downyflake held contests with cash prizes for the novelest and most nutritional way to eat donuts that could be purchased at its shops, like the two in Providence, and crafted into impressive desserts. It advertised the contests in national magazines and suggested that recipes like this one could win.

You don't have to be an expert cook. Just a new way of serving donuts, such as Peach Donut Shortcake, will win. Try it tonight…donuts sliced in half the long way, then covered with fresh sliced peaches and topped by whipped cream. A quick easy dessert, it's wholesome and delicious.

Downcity Diner Meatloaf
From Anthony Salemme

1 ½ pounds lean ground beef
¾ cup oats
¾ cup finely chopped onion
¾ cup tomato juice

1 egg, lightly beaten
¾ teaspoon salt
½ teaspoon black pepper

Heat oven to 350 degrees. Combine all ingredients in large bowl; mix lightly but thoroughly.

After mixing, form the meat into a loaf shape. Place on a greased baking pan and pour ¾ cup water around the meat.

Bake 50 to 55 minutes or until meatloaf is to medium doneness (160 degrees for beef, 170 degrees for turkey), until not pink in center and juices show no pink color. Let stand 5 minutes before slicing.

Top with brown gravy.

Brown Gravy
(No kidding, it's from a jar)

1 jar Heinz savory beef gravy

Heat until bubbly.

Bibliography

American Cancer Society, RI Division. *The Rhode Island Sampler.* Edited by Amy G. McCullough. Memphis: Wimmer Brothers, 1988.

Brown University Department of American Civilization. "John Rector Interview." *Underground Rhode Island.* December 12, 2003. Accessed September 18, 2018. https://repository.library.brown.edu/studio/item/bdr:147273.

Brussat, David. *Lost Providence.* Charleston, SC: The History Press, 2017.

Cianci, Vincent, and David Fisher. *Politics and Pasta.* New York: Thomas Dunne Books, 2011.

Corriea, Robert. "Waitress, 72, Feted For Her Four Decades of Service." *Providence Journal,* June 15, 1985.

Dexheimer, Dorothy A. "Miss Dutton Didn't Fail After All." *Providence Sunday Journal,* January 31, 1954.

Dutton, Flora. *Miss Dutton's Cookbook.* Swansea, MA: First Congregational Church of Swansea, 1957.

———. *Olde White Church Cook Book.* Swansea, MA: First Congregational Church of Swansea, 1967.

Eddy, Muriel E., and C.M. Eddy. *The Gentleman from Angell Street.* Narragansett, RI: Fenham Publishing, 2001.

Freedman, Paul. *Ten Restaurants that Changed America.* New York: Liveright Publishing Corporation, 2016.

Funderburg, Anne Cooper. *Sundae Best: A History of Soda Fountains.* Bowling Green, OH: Bowling Green State University Popular Press, 2002.

G.D.B. "In Perspective—A True Night Town When…" *Providence Journal*, July 1, 1967.

Gifford, Robert T. "The Shepard Company." National Register of Historic Places Nomination Form, Providence, Rhode Island, Downtown Providence Preservation Project, 1976.

Gunion, Philip C. "Frank Koerner to Dish Up His Last Meal." *Providence Evening Bulletin*, October 30, 1959.

Hall, Joseph D., Jr. *Biographical History of the Manufacturers and Business Men of Rhode Island*. Providence, RI: J.D. Hall & Co., 1901.

Hanlon, John. "Some Fond Recollections of Dining at Miss Dutton's." *Providence Evening Bulletin*, March 1, 1965.

Horvitz, Eleanor F. "Max Zinn and the Narragansett Hotel: The End of an Era." *Rhode Island Jewish Historical Notes* (Rhode Island Jewish Historical Association) 6, no. 3 (November 1973): 361–84.

Izenour, Steven. *White Towers*. Cambridge, MA: MIT Press, 1979.

Janusonis, Michael. "Joe's Upstairs: Looking Up Downtown." *Providence Journal*, January 19, 1976.

Lee, Donna. "Eddie & Son Dishes Up Homey Food, Atmosphere." *Providence Journal*, August 10, 1994.

Lee, Jennifer 8. *The Fortune Cookie Chronicles*. New York: Twelve, 2008.

Lovecraft, H.P. *Lord of a Visible World: An Autobiography in Letters*. Edited by S.T. Joshi and David E. Schultz. Athens: Ohio University Press, 2000.

Martin, Christopher Scott, and David Norton Stone. *Rhode Island Clam Shacks*. Charleston, SC: Arcadia Publishing, 2017.

McGowan, Louis, and Daniel Brown. Postcard History Series: *Providence*. Charleston, SC: Arcadia Publishing, 2006.

McVicar, D. Morgan. "New Restaurant Banking on City's Revival." *Providence Journal*, December 11, 1995.

O'Connell, James C. *Dining Out in Boston*. Hanover, NH: University Press of New England, 2017.

O'Gara, Eileen C., ed. *Divine Providence*. 2nd ed. Providence, RI: Brown University, 1986.

Providence Evening Bulletin. "Julienne's Is Closing; Owner Is Europe-Bound." August 1, 1980.

———. "Koerner's: A Haven that Soon May Be a Memory." June 6, 1983.

Providence Journal. "Fred H. Barrows Dead at His Home." May 3, 1941.

———. "Joe Schedley Steps Aside." n.d.

———. "Merchants' Opposition to Chinese Restaurants." February 4, 1917.

———. "Order to Chinese Restaurants." June 25, 1909.

———. "'Pie Alley' George Bellegris, 90, Lunchroom Owner, Dies." April 15, 1952.

———. "Protest Against Chinese Restaurant Not Sustained." March 6, 1917: 10.

———. "Would Bar Chinese Cafes on Westminster Street." July 16, 1916: 5.

Providence Sunday Journal. "Chinatown on the Move." December 13, 1914.

Raben, Jonathan D. *Italian Americans and Federal Hill.* Providence, RI: Seven Fishes Productions, 2006.

Rooke, John. *Rhode Island Radio.* Charleston, SC: Arcadia Publishing, 2012.

Rosenberg, Alan. "They Don't Mess with Pretension." *Providence Journal,* December 15, 1989.

Simster, Florence Parker. *Streets of the City: An Anecdotal History of Providence.* 3rd ed. Providence, RI: Mowbray Company, 1968.

Smith, Andrew F. *Encyclopedia of Junk Food and Fast Food.* Westport, CT: Greenwood Press, 2006.

Stanton, Mike. *The Prince of Providence.* New York: Random House, 2003.

Wheeler, Robert L. "Recalling These, Memory Grows Fonder." *Providence Journal,* December 3, 1939.

Wilber, Helen A. "A Light Lunch with Taste at Julie's Place." *Providence Journal,* June 8, 1974: W9.

Index

About the Author

David Norton Stone's lost restaurant credentials include working as a host at Panache and as a waiter for Michael's Catering after he graduated from Yale. For almost one full night, he washed dishes at a very famous (not lost) restaurant in Providence where, on the way out, he was told that he would never work in a restaurant in Providence again. That turned out to be true, so he went to law school. He has eaten at many of the lost Providence restaurants in this book and misses the meatball, fries and peppers plate at Eddie & Son, the salad bar at the Barnsider's Mile and a Quarter and the meatloaf sandwich (and everything else) at Downcity Diner. With his mother, he was lucky enough to eat at Buddy Cianci's Trapper John's during its brief run. His biggest lost restaurant regret is that he never tasted Ming Wings.

David first became interested in lost restaurants when his paternal grandmother, Helen, told him that she met his grandfather Norton on her way to Gibson's for a honeymoon sandwich one fateful lunch break from the Western Union during the Second World War. His maternal grandmother, Amelia, was a waitress at many Providence restaurants, including Johnson's Hummocks, and his grandfather Earl loved to dance at the Biltmore and spent many evenings at the Bacchante Room.

David is the author of the Rhode Island Quahog Trilogy: *Clamcake Summer*, *Stuffie Summer* and *Chowder Summer*. He is the coauthor of Images of America: *Rhode Island Clam Shacks*, and his food writing has appeared in *Rhode Island Monthly*, *Edible Rhody* and on Quahog.org. His work as a food historian has been cited by *Saveur* and *National Geographic*.